MINT TOWNS OF THE
BRITISH ISLES—SOUTH

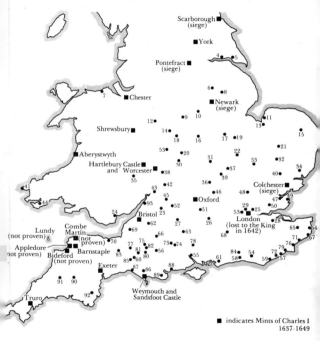

Scarborough
(siege)

■ York

Pontefract
(siege)

4

5

6   ■ 8

■ Newark
(siege)

7   ■ Chester

11

12   ■ 9   10

13

Shrewsbury ■

14   15

18   16   17   19

53   20   21

Aberystwyth ■   31   33   82

Hartlebury Castle   37   34
and Worcester ■

38   36   39   40

35   Colchester
(siege)

41   43   42   46   48   29   53   25   47   49

44   45   93   52   36   Oxford   51   26   London   28   50

24   (lost to the King   65   64
in 1642)

Bristol   23   62   66   63   68   61   58   54   59   71   67

69   70   77   75   81   73   74   78   72   76   79   57

Lundy   Combe   85   82   56   55   70   60
(not proven)   Martin
(not proven)   80   84

Appledore   88
(not proven)

Bideford   Barnstaple   87   86   89
(not proven)   Exeter

91   90   92

Truro ■   Weymouth and
Sandsfoot Castle

■ indicates Mints of Charles I
1637-1649

Map supplied by The Hamlyn Publishing Group

The Observer's Pocket Series

COINS

Observer's Books

NATURAL HISTORY
Birds · Birds' Eggs · Wild Animals · Zoo Animals
Farm Animals · Freshwater Fishes · Sea Fishes
Tropical Fishes · Butterflies · Larger Moths
Insects and Spiders · Pond Life · Sea and Seashore
Seashells · Dogs · Horses and Ponies · Cats
Trees · Wild Flowers · Grasses · Mushrooms · Lichens
Cacti · Garden Flowers · Flowering Shrubs
House Plants · Vegetables · Geology · Weather
Astronomy

SPORT
Association Football · Cricket · Golf · Coarse Fishing
Fly Fishing · Show Jumping · Motor Sport

TRANSPORT
Automobiles · Aircraft · Commercial Vehicles
Motorcycles · Steam Locomotives · Ships
Small Craft · Manned Spaceflight
Unmanned Spaceflight

ARCHITECTURE
Architecture · Churches · Cathedrals

COLLECTING
Awards and Medals · Coins · Postage Stamps · Glass
Pottery and Porcelain

ARTS AND CRAFTS
Music · Painting · Modern Art · Sculpture
Furniture · Sewing

HISTORY AND GENERAL INTEREST
Ancient Britain · Flags · Heraldry · European Costume

TRAVEL
London · Tourist Atlas GB

The Observer's Book of
COINS

HOWARD LINECAR

WITH BLACK AND WHITE PHOTOGRAPHS
AND DIAGRAMS IN THE TEXT

FREDERICK WARNE
LONDON

Published by
Frederick Warne (Publishers) Ltd
London, England
1977

© *Frederick Warne & Co Ltd 1977*

ISBN 0 7232 1564 2

Printed in Great Britain by
Butler & Tanner Ltd
Frome and London

CONTENTS

PREFACE

The purpose of this book, as of all others in the Observer's series, is to show the uninitiated some of the great interest that lies behind its subject. To most of us a coin is simply a piece of metal that will buy something. Few of us pause to consider how the piece of metal came into being. Nor do we realize the long story that lies behind the production of every coin.

In the first instance, someone had to design the coin. This design was then considered and when accepted a mint began the work of translating it into a coin. Most mints receive many more designs for any one coin than might be expected. The coin which we accept almost without thought is only the end product of the work of many skilled people.

It is also the purpose of this book to show something of the interest that lies behind the study and collection of coins as historic documents. Each coin is contemporary with its date of issue and thus reflects something of its own times. The story will be told as simply as possible, and should make the word 'numismatics', the science of coins and medals, appear a little less daunting.

Many books have already been written for the potential beginner in British coin collecting. Some of them take up the story as far back in history as 125 B.C., the approximate date when coins came into use in this country. A date so far back may well be beyond the interest of the beginner. This book therefore starts its account with coins that are familiar to most people and then traces their history backwards. A point is arrived at when the story can no longer be dealt with in this manner, but by that time the reader's interest will probably have been stimulated and he will be prepared to follow the matter into the more complicated early issues. It will be found that they have an interest that is all their own.

The value of money passes through periods of depreciation. Such a period exists at this time, but it has appeared many times before over the centuries. Such depreciations often bring into being alternative methods of transacting business. Cheques, bank notes and credit cards are some of these alternatives. It is thus sometimes argued that the day will come when coins may no longer be needed. Should this unlikely event happen, there will always be enough coins left in existence for the collector. Thousands of millions have been struck since coins first evolved some 700 years B.C. Though the majority are eventually called in and melted down enough will always survive for the enjoyment and instruction of the numismatist.

I wish to thank Mr Peter F. Davey for taking the photographs, the British Museum and Spink & Son Ltd, with whose permission they are reproduced.

Not all coins illustrated are full size.

H. W. A. Linecar

August 1976

1

DEFINITIONS

The condition of a coin will be dealt with in Chapter 6. There are some terms that will need explanation. Numismatic language is simple to understand given a few basic definitions.

Obverse The front or 'head' side of a coin. The obverse does not always show the head of the monarch. There were a few exceptions even in the days when kings and queens were plentiful. As the ruling houses of the world became fewer, democratic states frequently placed some form of a coat-of-arms or a national symbol on the obverse.

If a coin has a hole in the centre it usually does not show the head of the ruler. That would be considered an insult. Coins with such central piercings were usually minor denominations and frequently, as in British West Africa, issued to developing countries. The hole was in part intended to allow the coins to be threaded on a string to suit costumes which had no pockets.

Reverse The back or 'tails' side of a coin; often containing the coat-of-arms of the monarch, ruler or country. In more recent times local flora and fauna often appear. In some cases buildings and ships have been depicted. Even views of towns were used on some larger European pieces, but these are exceptions.

Blank The circular or other shaped piece of metal before it has been struck into a coin.

Flan The name given to the disc of metal after it has been struck. In North America it is often called the planchet.

Device The design which appears on the flan is frequently called the device. It is also sometimes called the design. The space on which the device appears is called the field.

Rim Most modern coins have a raised line of metal on both obverse and reverse round the perimeter of the flan. This is usually called the rim. It is intended to protect the rest of the coin from wear. It is therefore frequently slightly damaged, with cuts or nicks of a minute size. Some of these may be produced while the coin is passing through the various sorting and bagging processes immediately after being struck. Within the rim is frequently to be found a ring of dots. These are often called beads. Alternatively the dots may be of an elongated shape: they are then often called a 'toothed border', for want of a better description. Beads appear upon the 10 New Pence: there are not any on the 50p. They are becoming void of purpose on coins of no intrinsic value. Searchers for minute die varieties will sometimes count the number of beads or teeth. They can vary in number.

Edge The side of the coin when viewed thin-way on. The edge can be plain, can contain lettering known as the edge legend or can have graining with either vertical or twisted lines. The latter is sometimes called a 'cable' edge.

The original idea of the edge legend or graining was to protect the coin from being clipped. By clipping, a small amount of precious metal could be obtained which, when accumulated, could be sold as bullion. In Britain after 1662 any gold or silver coin with a smooth edge could be seen to have been clipped.

Edge legends and graining were adopted together in this country in 1662. The legend appeared on the larger coins, such as the Crown. It read DECUS ET TUTAMEN ANNO REGNI and a figure, meaning 'an ornament and a safeguard' (to the coin against clipping), 'in the ... year of our reign'. The Coronation Crown of Elizabeth II issued in 1953 had the legend in English, + FAITH AND TRUTH I WILL BEAR UNTO YOU.

With modern valueless coins graining has become a tradition which could be dispensed with. The 10 New Pence, derived from the Florin, has a grained edge. The 50 New Pence does not. At one period a security edge was devised. This consisted of two rows of graining with a peripheral groove, the groove extending behind the graining like a letter T. This complicated edge was intended to prevent silver coins issued in parts of the British Commonwealth from being forged by casting in a plaster mould. This type of forgery was extensive in the then Straits Settlements.

Legend   This is the lettering on the obverse, reverse and sometimes edge. The words are frequently abbreviated and in Britain are in part still in Latin. The obverse legend of the 50 New Pence reads ELIZABETH II D.G REG. F.D. and the date—except in the 1973 commemorative piece, when the date went on to the reverse. This is in full: Elizabeth II, Dei Gratia Regina Fidei Defensor, which translates as Elizabeth the Second by the Grace of God Queen, Defender of the Faith. The latter title was given to Henry VIII and was taken in as part of the Royal Title, being added to the legend on the coinage in 1715 (George I). As George I was German and spoke no word of English it was apparently considered politic to point out that he would uphold the British religion.

When describing a coin it is usual to write the legend in capital letters. An exceptional legend occurred on the Canadian 5 Cents from 1943 to 1945. It was in Morse code, took the place of the ring of dots, and read WE WIN WHEN WE WORK WILLINGLY.

Exergue On many coins, such as the British Sovereign, a small segment of the reverse is cut off below the design by a line from rim to rim. The date is frequently placed in the space so formed, the space being called the exergue and the line the exergual line.

Frosting Coins, particularly proof or pattern pieces, may be issued with certain parts of the design slightly dulled. This is usually called frosting, since it has that appearance. In the British series it can be found on coins from the seventeenth and eighteenth centuries onwards, but it is not common.

Mule The animal so named is the progeny of the horse and the donkey. The name is used by numismatists to signify a coin produced from two dies which do not normally belong together. An extreme example would be for the obverse of a 5 New Pence 1971 to be muled with the reverse of a Shilling. In 1936, the obverse of the East Africa 10 Cents was accidentally muled with the reverse of the 1936 Penny of British West Africa. Apart from such mistakes, mules can be intentional.

Mint marks and others Mint marks, sometimes also referred to as privy marks or initial marks, began to appear on the English hammered coinage in about the reign of Edward II (1307–27). In this reign the gold coins struck by the Bishop of Durham had their own mark by which they could be identified. By the reign

AN ALPHABETICAL CHART OF ENGLISH MINT MARKS

MINT MARK	SYMBOL	OCCURS IN REIGN OF
A		Elizabeth I
Acorn		Henry VIII, Elizabeth I
Anchor		Henry VII, Elizabeth I, Charles I, Commonwealth
Anchor and B		Charles I
Annulet		Edward IV
Annulet and pel-let		Edward IV, Henry VIII
Arrow		Henry VIII, Edward VI
Bell		Elizabeth I, James I, Charles I
Boar's head		Edward V, Richard III
Boar's head		Richard III
Boar's head		Charles I
Book		James I, Charles I
Bow		Edward VI
Br		Charles I
Castle		Henry VIII

Castle		Elizabeth I, James I, Charles I
Castle and H		Henry VIII
Catherine wheel		Henry VIII
Cinquefoil		James I
Cinquefoil		Edward IV, Henry VII
Coronet		Edward III, Henry IV, Edward IV, Philip and Mary, Charles I
Crescent		Elizabeth I, James I
Crescent		Henry VIII
Cross		Edward III
Cross: broken		Edward III
Cross		Edward III
Cross calvery		Charles I
Cross crosslet		Henry VII, Philip and Mary
Cross fleurée		Henry VI, Edward IV
Cross: Latin		Elizabeth I
Cross: long fit-chee		Edward IV, Henry VII, Henry VIII
Cross pattée		Edward III, Richard II, Henry IV, Henry V, Henry VI, Edward IV, Charles I

Cross and pellets		Edward IV
Cross: pellet in central piercing		Edward IV
Cross: pierced		Henry V, Henry VI, Edward IV
Cross: pierced and pellets		Edward IV
Cross: plain		Henry VI, Edward IV, Henry VIII, Elizabeth I, James I
Cross potence		Henry VI, Henry VIII
Cross potent		Edward III
Cross: Restoration		Henry VI
Cross: Saltire		James I
Cross: short fitchée		Henry VI, Edward IV
Cross: voided		Henry VI, Henry VIII
Crown		Charles I
Crozier		Edward III, Henry VII
Dragon		Henry VII
Eglantine		Elizabeth I
Ermine		Elizabeth I
Escallop		Henry VII, Henry VIII, Edward VI

15

Escallop		Elizabeth I, James I
Eye		Charles I
Flower & B		Charles I
Gerb		Charles I
Grapes		James I, Charles I
Grapple		Edward VI
Greyhound's head		Henry VII
Hand		Elizabeth I
Harp		Charles I
Heart		Charles I
Helmet		Charles I
Key		Henry VIII, Elizabeth I, James I
Leopard's head		Henry VII, Charles I
Lion		Edward VI, Elizabeth I, Charles I
Lion rampant		Charles I
Lis		Henry VI, Edward IV, Henry VII, Henry VIII, Edward VI, Philip and Mary, Elizabeth I, James I, Charles I

16

Lis		Henry VIII, Elizabeth I
Lis and rose dimidiate		Henry VII
Lis issuing from rose		Henry VII
Lis on rose		Henry VII
Lis on rose and sun		Henry VII
Martlet		Henry VII, Henry VIII, Edward VI, Elizabeth I
Mullet		Henry V, James I, Charles I
Mullet pierced		Edward VI, Elizabeth I
Negro's head		Charles I
Ostrich head		Edward VI
Pall		Edward IV
Pansy		Henry VII, Henry VIII
Pear		Charles I
Pheon		Henry VII, Henry VIII, Edward VI, Elizabeth I
P in brackets		Charles I
Plume		Charles I

17

Plume: Aberystwyth		Charles I
Plume: Oxford		Charles I
Plume: Shrewsbury		Charles I
Pomegranate		Henry VIII
Portcullis		Elizabeth I, Charles I
Portcullis crowned		Henry VIII
R in brackets	(R)	Charles I
Rose		Henry VI, Edward IV, Henry VII, Henry VIII, Edward VI, Elizabeth I, James I
Rose		Charles I
Sceptre		Charles I
Six (6)		Edward VI
Spur rowel		James I
Star		Henry VIII, Elizabeth I, Charles I
Star, rayout		Henry VIII
Sun		Edward IV
Sun		James I, Charles I, Commonwealth

Sunburst		Henry VIII
Sun halved		Edward IV, Edward V, Richard III
Sun halved		Richard III, Henry VII
Swan		Edward VI
Sword		Elizabeth I
T		Edward VI
T C		Edward VI
Thistle		James I
Trefoil		Henry VI, Edward VI, Henry VIII, Edward VI
Trefoil slipped		Henry VI, James I
Trefoil slipped		James I
Triangle		Charles I
Triangle in circle		Charles I
Tun		Henry VII, Edward VI, Elizabeth I, James I, Charles I
Woolpack		Elizabeth I
W.S.		Henry VIII, Edward VI
Y		Edward VI

(By courtesy of Spink & Son Ltd)

of Richard II seven marks were being used, and by the reign of Henry VII (1485–1509) these marks had begun to multiply.

They are usually placed at the beginning of the legend, in about the 12 o'clock position on the obverse and/or the reverse. As they developed, they were intended to convey certain information. In some cases the mark showed the place in which the coin had been struck. The dates during which a certain mint mark was used can show the period of time over which the coin had been struck. This does not mean that the same coin did not continue to be struck, but the mark was changed after a period of months or years. This sometimes signified the end of a particular journeyweight of coins produced. (See Trial of the Pyx, *below* p. 22.) The mint mark could also indicate the person who was responsible for the striking of the coin. A latter form of mark could show the place of origin of the metal from which the coin was struck.

A few examples may make the point clearer:

Edward II	Durham episcopal mark of Bishop Beaumont—a lion and Lis.
Richard II	Seven initial marks used.
Henry VII	Seventeen marks used by Tower Mint, three by provincial mints.
Elizabeth I	Thirty marks in use.
Charles I	Twenty-one marks in use at the Tower, others for provincial mints.

This brings us to the end of the use of mint marks on our hammered coinage. With the introduction of milled coinage the following marks have the significance listed:

Elephant, or elephant and castle = metal supplied by the Africa Company.

VIGO = metal said to have been captured at the Battle of Vigo Bay, 1702.

EIC = metal supplied by the East India Company.

LIMA = metal supplied in part from bullion captured by Admiral Anson in the Philippine Islands, amalgamated with other metal captured in the Atlantic.

A plume of feathers = metal from Welsh mines. (Also used on hammered coinage of Charles I.)

Rose = metal from West of England mines.

B = struck at Bristol temporary mint.

C = struck at Chester temporary mint.

E = struck at Exeter temporary mint.

N = struck at Norwich temporary mint.

Y or y = struck at York temporary mint.

Roses & plumes = metal supplied by the Company for smelting down lead.

WCC = metal from the Welsh Copper Company.

SSC = metal supplied by the South Sea Company.

Plumes = metal from the Company of Copper Miners in the Principality of Wales.

H = struck at the mint of Ralph Heaton & Co., Birmingham, as subcontractors to the Royal Mint, later The Mint, Birmingham, Ltd, now The Birmingham Mint, Ltd.

KN = struck by the Kings Norton Metal Company, Birmingham, as subcontractors to the Royal Mint.

Collectors who specialize in hammered coins do not necessarily agree that some of the above examples are 'mint marks'. Certainly those which indicate the source of the metal are not, but they are included here to obviate the use of a small separate section to accommodate them, and to help to indicate some points of this nature which the collector will encounter and should look for.

Privy marks, mentioned above, are not always mint marks. A privy mark may occur on a coin that also has a mint mark, mainly before the mint mark showed the dates on which a particular coin was issued. A privy mark may be concealed among the letters of the legend or elsewhere. It may take the form of an annulet (circle) or a broken annulet, or other forms. Such a mark was usually intended to show that coins so marked were struck during a particular period of weeks, months or years, indicating in some cases the journeyweight period during which the coin had been struck. At the annual Trial of the Pyx these coins could then be identified and pinned down to the time when they were struck or to the person responsible for striking them.

Trial of the Pyx This ancient Trial has the slight connection with mint marks just mentioned and is thus worthy of a short account. In remote times, if a moneyer issued forged, false or badly underweight coins, he was liable to suffer a penalty of personal mutilation. The idea was then formulated of appointing an outside body to inspect the coinage at intervals—to ensure its being up to standard in all respects. From each journeyweight of coins produced, specimens were set aside in a box called a Pyx. Eventually, the Worshipful Company of Goldsmiths became the body which inspected and tested the coins at the Trial and pronounced on their quality.

It is not known when the Trial was first instituted, but mention of such an event is made as far back as 1250. By about 1351 the Trial was taking place every three months. At this period a privy mark of the Master of the Mint's choosing was placed on the coins, the mark being changed every three months. By the time of Elizabeth I (1558–1603), the initial or mint mark itself became the privy mark and Edward VI (1547–53) had extended the period from three months to a year. It returned to a quarterly event for a time but finally settled at one year. This trial is still carried out each year—even though, apart from the Sovereign and the four Maundy coins, no precious metal coins are struck. The Goldsmiths, however, still keep an eye on the coinage.

Countermarks A countermark is placed on a coin for various reasons. It can take almost any form and is usually used to alter the exchange value of the coin, or to make that coin usable in circulation in a country other than that for which it was struck. Countermarks were used in considerable numbers in the early coinages in circulation in the West Indies. Usually the Spanish Eight Reales or Dollar was countermarked by the local government and put into circulation on a particular island. One such countermark was GR, put on various gold and silver coins for use in Jamaica, in 1758. Coins were also cut into sections which, with or without countermarks, were put into circulation as smaller denominations in the West Indies. In Britain, Spanish Dollars were countermarked with the head of George III and put into circulation in the early years of the nineteenth century.

Crosses A cross in many forms has always played a part in the design of our currency. It could have a religious significance, be used to mark coins in the Penny period for cutting into Halfpennies or Farthings before such were minted, or be just a pleasant form of design suitable in some subtle way to enhance the circular shape of the coin.

The hammered coinage period in this country was probably the most prolific in cross variety, when the following were used at various times.

The cross did not entirely disappear with the introduction of milled coinage. The four shields of arms

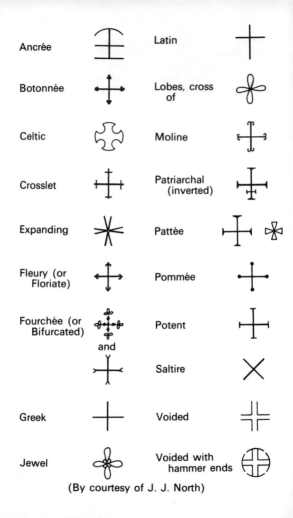

Ancrée		Latin	
Botonnée		Lobes, cross of	
Celtic		Moline	
Crosslet		Patriarchal (inverted)	
Expanding		Pattée	
Fleury (or Floriate)		Pommée	
Fourchée (or Bifurcated)	and	Potent	
Greek		Saltire	
Jewel		Voided	
		Voided with hammer ends	

(By courtesy of J. J. North)

were set in cruciform. This type of design lasted until the reign of Elizabeth II, where it appeared on the Coronation Crown of 1953. It appears to have gone out of use—at any rate for the present—on our decimal coinage, but will no doubt reappear in some form in time to come. A small cross is sometimes placed at the beginning or end of the legend. It was so used on the obverse of the first coins of Elizabeth II. In this form it may again appear at almost any time.

Rarity symbols need some explanation. These are quite simple: there are three scales in use.

With the first—

RRR = extremely rare
RR = very rare
R = rare
S = scarce
C = common

sometimes N = normal, neither rare nor common

This scale tends to be used for older coins, such as the English hammered series, where the exact number struck is usually never known and the rarity is assessed over the years by the number of specimens seen by collectors and dealers.

With later coinages, where numbers struck are frequently known, the second scale is often used. In this—

R7 = only one or two known
R6 = three or four known
R5 = five to ten known
R4 = eleven to twenty known
R3 = extremely rare (as RRR)
R2 = very rare (as RR)
R = rare
S = scarce
N = normal, neither scarce nor common

```
C  =common
C2 =very common
C3 =extremely common
```

A third rarity scale was devised by Wilson Peck for his British Museum Catalogue. *Copper, Tin and Bronze Coins in the British Museum, 1558–1958*. It was based on the fact that such minor denominations are usually struck in large numbers. This is particularly so in and after the reign of Victoria, when bronze coins after 1860 could be and often were struck in hundreds of millions. Collectors of copper and bronze coins therefore use the following scale of rarity—

```
EXC = Excessively common
EC  = Extremely common
VC  = Very common
C   = Common
S   = Scarce
VS  = Very scarce
R   = Rare
VR  = Very rare
ER  = Extremely rare
EXR = Excessively rare
PU  = Probably unique
```

It will be noted that this scale works the opposite way round from those given above. This is of no importance: it is a good and well-considered scale for the coins with which it deals.

Treasure trove The rights and wrongs of the unlicensed sale and use of metal detectors is no part of this work. There is just the possibility that one of these machines may bring to light a hoard of coins. Hoards also come to light during building excavations and during agricultural work.

The English law on the subject can be fairly simply

stated. If a coin or hoard of coins is found and the coins are of gold or silver they are likely to be treasure trove. Such a find must be reported to the police, who will contact the local Coroner.

The Coroner will then hold an inquest on the find, at which the jury, or in some cases the Coroner himself, will determine:

(1) Whether the find is of silver and/or gold.
(2) On the evidence produced, whether the find was lost by accident, abandoned or deliberately concealed.
(3) Who is the owner: if known, the find is not treasure trove.
(4) Who was the finder.
(5) Whether there was any concealment of the find.

If the verdict is that the coins are treasure trove the Coroner will formally seize it for the Queen. This simply means that he places it in the possession of HM Treasury. In fact it will go to the British Museum, where the Department of Coins and Medals will record the find-spot and catalogue the coins. The general rule laid down is that finders who report their discoveries will receive back the coins, apart from those required by the Museum or other recognized institutions (such as a museum close to the find-spot). It is not binding in law, but it is the usual practice for the Museum to pay the full market value for the coins retained.

All or any of the coins returned to the finder are his property to do with as he likes. The Museum will advise the owner of reliable dealers or auctioneers through whom the coins may be sold.

Coins in metals other than gold and silver are not treasure trove, but the finder will be doing a service to archaeology by reporting his find. All find-spots are carefully noted and mapped and may have a significance quite unrealized by the finder. Treasure trove also includes other objects in gold and silver, apart from coins.

A Licence must usually be obtained to legalize diving for coins and other objects to be found in ships wrecked off the coast within territorial waters. Any such finds must be reported to the Receiver of Wrecks. Full details about the English law of treasure trove were epitomized in an article by Mr J. D. Wheeler in *The Numismatic Circular*, October 1974, pp. 389–90, published by Spink & Son, from which account the above facts are taken.

2

IT STARTED WITH A PENNY

The majority of people look briefly at the coins they use every day, but they fail to observe them closely or ask questions about them. A brief glance at the size of the coin and at its shape tells the user its value. Some men run a finger round the edge of a coin while it is still in their pocket. If the edge is grained, it is a 5 or 10 Penny piece. If the edge is smooth it is a bronze 2 Pence; if small, a Penny or Halfpenny. In 1937, when the 12-sided Threepence first made its appearance, the feel of its shape and thickness told at once what coin it was. The seven-sided 50 Pence is distinguishable by touch from the 10 Pence, in spite of their similarity in size.

Many people deal with coins in this way, almost without thought. Yet a number of artists submitted many designs for our various decimal denominations. These were considered by the Royal Mint Advisory Committee, who eliminated one design after another until finally our New Pence came into being.

When we had become familiar with them we thought little more about them, yet there is much of interest in our coinage. A considerable history lies behind it, and once this is considered, the interest of the individual is aroused. He or she has taken the first step towards becoming a collector of coins. A single example, the one New Penny, is a good starting-point. Our pound now consists of 100 pence; this is the latest development of our most historic coin, the Penny.

All but the very young can remember the bronze Penny, with the head of the Queen on the obverse and Britannia seated on a rock, on the reverse. With various minor alterations, such as the presence or absence of a ship and lighthouse on the reverse, the Penny had been of this type since 1860—*i.e.* through the second half of the reign of Victoria (1837–1901), and the reigns of Edward VII (1901–10), George V (1910–36), Edward VIII (1936), George VI (1936–52) and the first years of the present reign. It was displaced when decimalization was adopted on 15 February 1971.

For the first half of the reign of Victoria the Penny had been struck in copper and was even larger than the bronze piece. Basically, its design was much the same. Because of its weight and size, and the high price of copper, the coin was struck in bronze from 1860. It had been a copper piece since its introduction in 1797.

As a 'copper' it had been struck through the second half of the reign of George III (1760–1820), and the reigns of George IV (1820–30) and William IV (1830–37). When it first appeared in 1797, it soon earned for itself the name of 'cartwheel', on account of its size and the raised rim round the edge. By the time of the second issue in 1806 it had lost its ponderous appearance. Thus, with four main variations in size, metal and weight, the Penny gradually contracted into the one New Penny of today.

But the story of the Penny goes much farther back than 1797. It is the oldest coin we have, and was first introduced into this country about A.D. 765 when Heahberht was King of Kent, and England was divided into several kingdoms.

At this far-off time the Penny was a silver coin, which

varied in size from approximately that of our present 5 New Pence to that of the pre-decimal Sixpence. It was very thin and was struck by hand. Coins so struck are known as hammered pieces; why this is so will be explained in due course. The Penny continued to be our only coin until the reign of Edward I (1272–1307), when a larger silver piece called a Groat or 'great piece', value four pence, made its first tentative appearance. In spite of the larger Groat and of a gold coinage first introduced for general use in the reign of Edward III (1327–77), the silver Penny remained. It is the only coin we still have that has been struck in every reign, in either silver, or copper or bronze, from 765 to 1975. Gold Nobles, Pounds and Sovereigns, silver Crowns, Halfcrowns and Florins came and went; the Penny remained.

After the first appearance of the Penny in copper, the silver coin from which the new piece had been derived continued to be struck. Though greatly reduced in size, it now formed part of a set of four coins—Penny, Twopence (Half-groat), Threepence and Fourpence (or Groat, the name still lingers). Sets of these are distributed by or for the monarch on Maundy Thursday to as many poor people as the monarch has years of age.

This ancient ceremony is still carried out each year. The four coins which the present Queen usually distributes in person are still struck in silver, are legal tender (though no one would think of spending them) and the smallest of them is the Penny. In its present form only very few specimens of the Penny and the other three denominations are struck. When the Queen was 40 years of age, 40 men and 40 women pensioners each received 40 pence, made up of the four denominations mentioned. Thus less than 2000 of each denomination are struck each year, making these little silver coins somewhat rare. For this reason alone they are never spent; they are real collector's pieces. The pensioners also receive a further sum of money in lieu of clothing and food which was once distributed in kind. A Crown piece once worth 60 pence, but now nominally worth 25 pence, is usually included with this cash. Thus the Penny continues in use in two forms.

The early hammered pieces form a collecting theme in themselves. They were struck for the various Anglo-Saxon kings for the kingdoms of Kent, Mercia, Wessex, East Anglia and Northumbria, and for the Archbishops of Canterbury and York. They were also copied by the Viking invaders, who received many of them as Danegeld. Considerable numbers of English Pennies are therefore to be found in Scandinavian museums.

They were of many types, often containing a crude representation of the head or bust of the monarch. Of particular interest is the fact that the moneyer, the man responsible for striking the coins, though he was not always the man who did the actual work, was, as time passed, ordered to put his name on the coin. Usually, this appeared on the reverse, while the name of the king appeared on the obverse.

The actual bust, lettering and other design on the coin was built up by the use of a series of punches which can often be analysed and grouped: hair, eyes, crowns, nose and the like, with various dots, curves, crosses and strokes which built up into letters. The coin developed in detail but altered little in style, as the 'portrait' was conventional, and not intended to be a likeness.

By the time of the unification of the kingdoms in about A.D. 955 (the date and the identity of the first king to rule all England is still a point of some argument), Pennies were being struck at many mints throughout the country. The name of the mint town had also begun to appear on the coin, usually in abbreviated form. During the period 973–1066 some 87 towns had their own mints. It is possible, therefore, to collect these early Pennies under town names and it is interesting to note how old many of our towns are. They were small places then and some of them still are, by modern standards. They clustered in that part of the country which lies south of a line from Land's End to York, with Shrewsbury and Chester just north of the line. All this information has been the subject of research and cataloguing: the towns with mints, the moneyers who struck the Pennies in each town, how some of the moneyers moved about from one town to another, and the kings who ruled during the various periods.

When William I (1066–87) conquered the country he continued this monetary system. During the Norman period of our history some 76 mints struck Pennies. The mint towns now reached northward to Newcastle, Durham and Carlisle. In the main, types and styles remained basically the same.

By the time the first Plantagenet king, Henry II (1154–89), came to the throne, the long period of about 500 years during which the Penny was our only coin was drawing to its close. Increasing trade with Europe called for coins of higher denomination, such as the Groat already mentioned. By the time of Edward III (1327–77) a coinage in gold was established and the complications of our coinage began.

The chronicle of events behind what might be called the 'Penny period' of our numismatic history is immense. It comes to life as one handles the actual coins used in England in those far-off times. The various kings and rulers cease to be an irritating series of faceless beings to be learnt and dimly understood at school. The breath of life comes into them; they take on a personality, and the whole historic scene becomes animated. Men cutting small pieces of silver into discs and striking them into coins in every important town in the country appear as personalities, many moving from mint to mint as occasion demanded, through a country in which it was still relatively dangerous to travel. There were only a few poor roads and trackways, some inherited from the Romans. The country was still deeply afforestated. One thing that would certainly strike us above all others, if we were able to return to this period of history, would be the silence of a non-mechanical world.

Before we leave the Penny as a subject, one point might be made. Over the centuries, coins of larger denomination—usually struck in gold—have been called the unit of coinage. The present unit is the Sovereign, another name for the British Pound, or Pound sterling. Before decimalization the Pound was made up of 240 pennies; now it is composed of 100 pence, the value of the Penny having been uprated by the change. Thus the real unit from which all other British coins have sprung is really the Penny. For as long as Britain maintains its own coinage, separate from all other countries, or from a possible coinage for the Common Market countries, this is likely to remain the case. All our decimal denominations and those which preceded them, the Crown, Halfcrown, Florin, Shilling, Sixpence, Fourpence, Threepence (in silver and base metal) and the Twopence, together with the Half Sovereign which was once, like the Sovereign, in general use, are all multiples of the Penny. It is right, therefore, that this one name alone should have been carried forward through our latest great coinage change.

We can now move on to observe something of our various gold coinages and, as with the Penny, will study their history from the present Sovereign backwards in time.

3

SOVEREIGNS AND GOLD

It will probably surprise many readers to learn that in this day and age of austerity and inflation the Royal Mint is still striking gold Sovereigns of the same fineness, size and weight as those which it struck in 1817 (George III). In its present form, the Sovereign was reintroduced into the range of coins when an earlier reformation of our coinage was undertaken. It had appeared previously in the reign of Henry VII (1485–1509) as a hammered coin. The name was later dropped in favour of other names for a piece of similar value. Before we trace back the origins of British gold coinage a word of explanation of the apparent anomaly of the continuance of striking Sovereigns should be given.

The Pound (=Sovereign) is the internationally recognized unit of our coinage. When it was introduced in its present form in 1817 the amount of gold in the coin would buy the equivalent in goods or services. This situation continued, at any rate in theory, until Britain went off the gold standard in the early 1930s. The First World War had seen the Sovereign replaced by paper notes, the striking of the coin being suspended. When Britain no longer based its money on a gold standard it meant, in basic terms, that if a Pound Note were tendered at the Bank of England, which had issued it, the Bank would not give one gold Sovereign in return.

This is where, in part, inflation began to affect the economy. The final result was that the coins which we use today have no intrinsic value at all, being simply tokens backed in part by a gold reserve.

There are several reasons why Sovereigns are still being struck. They are still technically legal tender for one pound, though changing hands at anything up to 30 times that value, and containing far more than one pound's worth of gold. The curious situation arises that citizens of this country cannot obtain this form of legal tender except through a coin dealer, at a premium. There are many countries in the Middle East, Greece, Turkey and others, who still respect the British Sovereign and keep their personal savings in this coin. They also carry out business transactions with it. As a piece of bullion it is still dealt with in Europe, and is frequently to be had from Swiss banks. The striking of gold into coin calls for certain skills and knowledge. For this reason also, the Royal Mint is glad to be in a position to continue striking. These complications are really outside our brief, but are offered in explanation

The student of coins, the collector, is not primarily concerned with these economic questions. To the collector, the Sovereign is a coin, a collector's piece, with a history as rich in information as that of the Penny.

The coinage reform which was undertaken in 1816/ 17 had become necessary for a number of reasons, mainly those of complicated economics. The Royal Mint, which had for some six hundred years been located in the Tower of London, was constantly under pressure from the army, which needed the whole of the available space within the ramparts. The Mint machinery was in a poor state and the whole organization needed overhaul. After some years of deliberation it was decided to erect a new mint on the site on Tower Hill where it now stands. The work has now been transferred to the latest Royal Mint at Llantrisant in Wales, but Tower Hill was still busy until a few months ago.

When the Tower Hill buildings were ready for occupation they were fitted out with new steam-driven coining machinery by Boulton and Watt of Soho, Birmingham, and the reformed coinage began to be struck. It consisted of a Sovereign and Half Sovereign in gold, a Crown, Halfcrown, Shilling and Sixpence in silver, together with the four silver pieces of Maundy Money. It should be mentioned here that the Threepence, which originally had the figure 3 on the reverse, was redesigned for general circulation in 1927/28 and continued in use alongside the 12-sided piece of 1937 until 1945.

With the reformed coinage of 1816/17, provision was made for Five-Pound and Two-Pound pieces to be struck in gold. These appeared only at long intervals and it is doubtful if they ever circulated.

The Sovereign first appeared in 1817 and was put into circulation at the value of one pound. At the same time gold was made the sole standard measure of value and the only legal tender for sums over two pounds. It replaced the Guinea. This coin was first put into circulation in 1663 (Charles II, 1660–85) after a previous coinage reform which will be dealt with later. The Guinea had fluctuated in value since its introduction and in 1817 settled at 21 shillings. As a name it continued to be used in trade and for paying fees, until decimalization.

The earlier coinage reform just mentioned took place in 1662. In that year, after a number of earlier experiments dating back to Elizabeth I (1558–1603), mill coinage was finally adopted.

Mill or milled coinage took its name from the fact that parts of the machinery used in its production were driven by wind, water or horse mills. At the English mint in the Tower a horse gin was used to drive the

37

rolling mills through which the metal passed several times to reduce it to the required thickness for striking into coins. The reason for the adoption of mill coinage was that the coins could be struck thick enough to have either a legend or graining (sometimes referred to as milling) on their edges. This protected them from being clipped, a dishonest method of removing a little metal from the edge—an evil which had long been in existence.

The Guinea took its name from the fact that the metal from which it was struck came in part from the Guinea or Gold Coast area of West Africa. Much of the metal was imported by the Africa Company, part of whose arms, an elephant and castle, sometimes appeared under the bust of the king. Five- and Two- Guinea pieces were also struck but, as with the Five-Pound piece, it is doubtful if the larger piece was ever much used in circulation.

The coinage reform of 1662 therefore brought into being the following coins: in gold—Five, Two, One and Half Guineas; in silver—Crown, Halfcrown, Shilling, Sixpence, Fourpence, Threepence, Twopence and Penny. All were multiples of the Penny and it is probable that it was at this stage in our coinage history that the silver coins of Fourpence to Penny first became used solely for Maundy Money. A number of copper, and in some cases tin, Halfpennies and Farthings were brought into use. They never met the demand for small change, a demand which in the end brought forth the copper coinage of 1797.

It will be appreciated that the three types of coinage with which we have been dealing so far in this chapter, that from 1662 until 1816, that from 1816 until 1971, and the present decimal coinage, all consisted of a compact and simple series of denominations, easy to use and simple to understand. It has, therefore, been simple to trace our coinage history backwards from the present. It would be inadvisable to attempt this with the coinage which was replaced in 1662.

This earlier series is known as the hammered coinage and stemmed in part from the Penny which we first examined. To deal with this hammered coinage it is necessary to go back to the introduction of our gold coinage and to deal with the whole story in a new chapter.

4

OUR HANDMADE COINAGE

Before we consider the origins of our gold coinage it might be well to say something of the way in which hammered coins were produced. Only slight reference has been made so far to this subject.

To produce a hammered coin various processes had to be carried out. Two dies were cut in hard metal—the hardest that could be obtained at any one period of time. The metal is usually called steel, but it has to be borne in mind that steel as we know it is a fairly modern development.

Steel is composed of iron and carbon. When a pure ore, such as the magnetic oxide of iron, and a nearly pure carbon, such as wood-charcoal, are used in its production the manufacture of steel of a reasonably fine quality is fairly simple. The ancient iron-makers obtained their steel from these components; it is therefore clear why so much reference in history is made to the charcoal-burner.

Coin dies were cut in this early form of steel. The device was engraved by hand with graving tools and punches of the type already mentioned (on page 32). As time passed the punches became more sophisticated until a point was reached when one punch might contain the whole bust of the monarch. Eventually one master punch was used and many dies were made from

1. An early mint, striking hammered coins. From the left: operator cutting blanks to size; furnace; scales for weight checking; operator beating sheet metal to correct thickness; official, possibly the Mint Master explaining the accounts to a visitor, possibly a prince or ruler; moneyer striking coins; apprentice placing blanks between the dies; basket for finished coins; strongbox, probably the pyx into which representative coins were placed for later testing at the Pyx Trial, now carried out by the Goldsmiths Company.

2. Blondeau's machine for rolling-on edge lettering or graining. The coins revolved between suitably marked bars. Most accounts agree that the coin blank was edge-marked before striking. The basket, (d), full of finished coins was probably 'artist's licence'. System adopted in Britain in 1662. (**1**.)

3. The 'horse-power' that drove the early rolling mills, *circa* 1662. (**1**.)

4. Money scales and weights for checking clipped, debased, counterfeit or foreign coins in the normal course of business. (**2**.)

5. Pair of dies for a hammered coin. Left, the reverse die which took the hammer blow. Right, the obverse die with ruler's portrait. Note tail for driving die into block of wood. *See* 1. (**3**.)

6. The healing properties of money! Charles II is pictured above touching a patient to relieve the 'king's evil' (scrofula). After the ceremony the sovereign presented the sick with a piece of his coinage to be hung around the neck—these were known as 'touchpieces'.

it. How long this progression took is not firmly established, but it is thought probable that one punch was used to produce the whole of the bust of Elizabeth I on her coinage.

The dies of the Pennies were, as we have seen, relatively simple. Next a piece of sheet silver, hammered to the required thickness, was cut by hand to a roughly circular shape. It was weighed and filed to the correct weight. It was then ready for striking.

The obverse die was placed in a solid base. A heavy baulk of timber was commonly used. This die frequently had a pointed end so that it could be driven into the wood. As the obverse die with the portrait of the monarch was the most difficult to produce, it was always placed as the lower die since it would thus suffer less during striking. This custom obtained at the Royal Mint at least until the mid-twentieth century.

The reverse die had a flat tail. The flan of metal was placed on the lower die and the upper die positioned upon it. Various types of rim which later developed into a collar held the dies in place one with another. The moneyer then struck the upper die with a hammer. The metal 'flowed' under the blow into the crevices of the die, producing the device on the coin.

To return to our gold coinage—a few Pennies had been struck in that metal. Probably the first example, equal in value to 20 silver pence, was minted in 1257, in the reign of Henry III (1216–72), right at the end of the 'Long Cross' penny period. Why this was done has never been quite clear. Some students think it was for the convenience of paying tribute exacted by the Roman Catholic Church. A few gold Pennies were easier to transport to Rome than a large number of silver pieces. It will be remembered that thousands of Pennies were needed to pay the Danegeld.

Very few examples of these gold Pennies still exist.

If they were for the purpose suggested they were probably melted down in Rome, the metal being used for the striking of other coins. Another school of thought suggests that these gold Pennies were an experiment, an attempt to produce a gold coin with a 10 to 1 ratio with the silver.

It was in the reign of Edward III (1327–77) that gold was again regularly coined. It had not been coined regularly since the seventh century, during which period the Anglo-Saxons had struck gold coins known as 'Thrymsas' in very small quantities. Edward, faced by an economic crisis, attempted its solution with gold.

The first coins, somewhat tentative, were a Florin, a Half-florin, also called a Leopard from the animal on the obverse, and a Quarter-florin. This was also called a Helm, from the helmet surmounted by a leopard on the obverse. These three pieces were struck between January and August 1344. They were designed by two Florentine goldsmiths whose names translated into Nicholyn and Kirkyn. The florin was proclaimed by Edward as a 'piece of two "Leopards" to be the weight of two Florentine florins and to circulate for six shillings'. The Half-florin or Leopard was to weigh the same as one Florentine florin and to circulate at three shillings. This quotation from accepted works on our coinage is, strictly, incorrect since the Shilling had not yet been evolved. In fact the English gold Florin was equivalent to 72 Pennies and the Half-florin to 36.

Part of the object of the exercise was to prevent the exportation of silver money from England. The brief period of circulation will have been noted; the three gold pieces were discontinued on 9 July 1344. A royal proclamation of 20 August made them acceptable only as bullion. More than one such mistake has been made in our coinage over the centuries.

Two points should be made here. First, coins were

in the very first instance derived from weights. The weight of metal in a coin settled its exchange value. Very broadly this continued for as long as precious metal coins were struck. Variations were obtained by increasing the amount of alloy. When this rule was abandoned coins became simply tokens. Thus our modern cupro-nickel coinage has of itself no value at all.

Secondly, the name Florin never appeared again among our coins until it was revived in 1849 (Victoria). It was then given to a silver piece value two shillings, 24 pence or one-tenth of a pound. The value of the pound was then 20 shillings or 240 pence. The coin was an attempt at decimalization, for which agitation had been going on for many years. It brought no result beyond the introduction of this one coin. Full decimalization had to wait until 1971, by which time British coinage was almost the only money remaining whose denominational ratios were not 10 to 1. In fact Britain was pushed into decimalization by isolation.

After the gold Florin had failed, Edward—in late 1344—proclaimed a coin to be called a Noble, having a ratio of 12 to 1 with silver. This experiment was reasonably successful and our gold coinage was now established.

The Noble was one of the very finest examples of the coin engraver's art. It was said to be so named because it was struck in the most noble of the metals. The king standing in a ship is thought to refer to the great naval victory of Sluys in 1340 when, in the wars against the French, 230 ships were taken during England's attempts to keep possession of our territories in Europe. It may be remembered that this series of campaigns contained the Battle of Crécy in 1346 and brought the king's son, Edward the Black Prince, prominently into history. If the Noble did refer to Sluys it was one of the world's first commemorative coins. Britain's first was probably the memorial coinage by the Danish settlers struck *c.* A.D. 890–905, in memory of Edmund (858–70). Britain's latest was the 25 Pence of 1973, commemorating the Silver Wedding of the Queen and Prince Philip, and the 50 Pence of the same year marking Britain's entry into the 'Common Market'.

Gold and silver coinage now circulated together and continued to do so for some six centuries. Many names such as Noble, Angel, Ryal, Unite, Pound and Sovereign were used for our gold coinage. With most of these denominations there were halves and frequently quarters. A list is given by reign in Chapter 10. One of the names most used was Sovereign, usually for a piece whose value was one pound or 240 pence.

The Sovereign first made its appearance in the reign of Henry VII (1485–1509). It continued to be struck until 1604 (James I, 1603–25), when the name disappeared until 1817. In the list of denominations it may be noted that there was a gold Crown, introduced in the reign of Henry VIII, and that this coin, like the Penny, later came to be struck in a less precious metal, silver. It will also be seen that our coinage, in spite of the complications of many names, continued on a fairly steady basis until the Civil Wars of Charles I (1625–49) when the whole coinage picture was upset. To many collectors and students this is our most colourful coinage period, one to be studied in depth, and one in which some questions still remain to be answered. Great detail cannot be given here, but a few leads to the interest of this coinage need to be included.

As soon as the Civil War broke out, when Charles raised his standard at Nottingham on 22 August 1642, the Royal Mint, located in the Tower, was at once lost to the king. The City of London, as most of the eastern side of England, declared against the king. One effect was that the king could not obtain money in coin from his Mint. In part this contingency had been foreseen; the king and his adherents were not fools.

A reasonable amount of silver and small amounts of gold were still being mined in Wales. Some of the silver mines had been flooded out. Sir Thomas Bushell convinced the government, and in particular the king, that he could drain certain of these mines and work to a greater depth. Bushell was the engineer-speculator of the period. He obtained permission to go ahead with his scheme. The silver which he extracted was, at his suggestion, coined into money at a mint set up for the purpose at Aberystwyth. With a number of technicians from the Tower Mint, Aberystwyth went into operation in 1638, four years before the Civil War began. As soon as the war started, the mint at which the metal could be coined was moved to Shrewsbury. Since, as has been explained, no fixed machinery was needed to strike hammered coins, a mint could be moved at will.

From the Parliamentary point of view the supporters of Cromwell, with the Tower Mint behind them, were able to produce all the money needed to support their cause. As the king was still king, even the Parliamentarians dared not produce their own coinage. The Tower continued to strike coins showing the king on the obverse. To have produced a new rebel coinage was to risk its not being accepted.

The king and his supporters had to provide money to pay those who fought for them. As the tide of war ebbed and flowed mints were set up at York, 1642–4; Aberystwyth (reinstated January to March 1646, though some of the coins may have been struck at Combe Martin between 1647 and 1648); Shrewsbury, 1642; Oxford, 1642–6; Bristol 1643–5; Truro, 1642–3; Exeter, 1643–6; Weymouth, 1643–4 (though the coins may have been struck at Sandsfoot Castle nearby);

Worcester, 1646 (the coins probably being struck in Hartlebury Castle near Kidderminster, since this was the seat of the Bishop of Worcester); and Chester, 1644.

The metal for these provincial mint coins came from various sources. A certain amount of gold was still struck, Shrewsbury and Oxford producing a Triple Unite or Three-Pound piece, the largest gold coin by size in the English series. Some silver came from Wales, or from Combe Martin, but much of the money was coined from domestic silver plate which the king 'borrowed', promising to repay when better times returned—which they never did.

In the more opulent families at this period silver plate was in reasonably common domestic use. China plates and dishes had not yet been developed; pewter was the usual alternative, with wood. Many great families, such as the Rashleighs, donated a chest of plate to the Royal cause. When the king settled his headquarters at Oxford, 1643–6, the college plate suffered irretrievably from his 'borrowing'. (Cambridge, it is said, came off better. They hid their plate and did not donate it to the Parliamentary cause.)

The movement of mints on the Royalist side gave rise to many most interesting coins. Apart from such unusual coins as the gold Triple Unite, and the silver Pound struck at Shrewsbury, the more usual denominations were maintained. It is known that mint technicians in some cases cut dies for both sides, but in many cases the coins produced were of rough workmanship, struck under stress and with little time to give to the niceties of production. It therefore follows that the many issues of this period abound in major varieties of design and are the subject of considerable interest and study. Most of them carried a mint mark to show where they had been struck.

This was not the end of the interesting complications

of the Civil War coinages. Certain towns were besieged. Here money was hastily struck to pay the defenders. Nothing undermines the morale of an army more than to receive no pay. Once more domestic plate was requisitioned, cut into many rough shapes and issued as money. In some rare cases hallmarks or parts of the design of the original silver vessel can be seen on the 'siege pieces'. Most of the besieged towns, such as Carlisle, Colchester, Newark and Pontefract, struck coins of usual denominational values. The shapes were often diamond or octagonal. Scarborough produced some 22 denominations with such unusual values as five shillings and eightpence, three shillings and fourpence, one shilling and threepence, elevenpence, and the like. These unusual denominations were decided by the intrinsic value of the roughly shaped pieces of silver from which they were made. This brings us back to the point that coins are primarily derived from weights. In the above cases the weight of silver settled the value of the coin, however odd.

Only a lead has been given to the great interest of the Civil War coinage. Once war breaks out, civil or international, strange things can happen to coins. Numerous different metals, odd denominations, various shapes and sizes and endless varieties of design can result. It had happened before in the world—it has happened since. The coins of the besieged towns of Europe over the centuries could form a research and collecting theme in themselves.

A little more of the story of our coinage needs to be dealt with to complete that of the hammered period. After the execution of Charles I, hammered and mill coins were struck for the Commonwealth, under Cromwell. When Charles II (1660–85) succeeded to the throne, hammered coins were still issued while preparations for the change to mill money as the sole type were in progress. In 1662, as we have seen, hammered coins ceased to be struck and 'modern' coinage came into being.

In the briefest possible way the story of our coinage has been outlined. A few points of interest to the collector have been indicated. If sufficient interest has been aroused it is obvious that many collecting themes exist and much informative study can be undertaken. The reader has been shown, it is hoped, that coins are not a dry-as-dust subject but are full of interest, history and colour. Let us now consider how they may be collected.

7. Gold stater of Philip II of Macedon, *c* 340 B.C. Increasingly copied as coins spread in the then known world: eventually reached Britain in very run-down form. (**4**.)

8. Ancient British bronze coin of Cunobeline, *c* A.D. 10–40, probably struck at *Camulodunum* (Colchester). (**4**.)

9. Bronze coin of Hadrian, A.D. 117–138, the emperor who caused the wall named after him to be built. Note Britannia on reverse, her first appearance on a coin, representing the Roman province of Britain. (**5**.)

10. A further bronze coin of Hadrian. The lady represents the African provinces, notably Egypt. (**5**.)

11. Silver decadrachm of Syracuse, *c* 412 B.C. Struck as a prize-coin for the victors in the annual Assinarian Games. (**6**.)

12. Coin of Nero, one of the most familiar names among the Roman emperors. (**5**.)

13. Gold, early Irish ring money, weight, 82·4 grains. Similar types used elsewhere.

14. Silver penny of Offa, king of Mercia (A.D. 757–96). The portrait is remarkable for this early period. (**7**.)

15. Silver penny of Æthelred II (A.D. 978–1016), one of the early kings of all England. Struck at Ipswich, one of over 100 mints in use in early times. (**8**.)

16. Silver penny of Harold II (Jan.–Oct. 1066) Known as the PAX type. (**8**.)

17. Silver penny of William I, the Conqueror (1066–87). Known as the sword type. (**8**.)

18. Silver penny of William II (1087–1100), known as the cross voided type from the cross on reverse. (**8**.)

19. Silver groat of Edward I (1272–1307), equal to 4 pennies. The king's titles include DI: GRA=by the grace of God (king), still used as D.G, and DVX AQVT=Duke of Acquitaine. The inner reverse legend shows the coin to have been struck in London. (**9**.)

20. Gold florin of Edward III (1327–77). An early attempt at an English gold coinage which failed. Note the great detail of the design. (**9**.)

21. Edward replaced the florin with a gold noble. The king standing in a ship is said to commemorate the naval victory over the French at Sluys, 1340, where the king commanded in person: thus one of the world's oldest 'commemorative' coins. (**7**.)

58

22. Silver crowns (5/-) were introduced in 1551 by Edward VI (1547–53) and have been struck since then till the 1977 crown of 25p in cupro-nickel. Here is one of Edward's half-sister, Elizabeth I (1558–1603). The initial mark 1 dates it at 1601.

23. As trade expanded with the discovery of the Far East and America the Spanish eight reales was accepted everywhere. Jealous of this Elizabeth gave her merchant venturers the piece of eight testerns in 1600 (0). Overseas merchants would not accept it, though it was struck over a Spanish piece of eight. (**10**.)

5

HOW ARE COINS COLLECTED?

Coins are collected, very broadly, for two reasons—interest and profit. Coin collectors can, again very broadly, be put into two categories—the student collector and the investor collector.

The student collector, the numismatist, is the backbone of real coin collecting. He builds his collection on a theme of historical interest that has a special appeal. The coins which he collects are illustrations of a great background of history and are a part of that history in which he takes an interest.

The collector of the coins of Ancient Greece, who does not necessarily have to be a classical student, appreciates their fine artistic merit and sees through his coins the background against which the coins were produced He sees the ancient world built of a number of Greek city states, each reasonably self-supporting, striking their own coinage. He sees these states fighting each other, failing to combine into a single nation of authority and power. Through his coins the collector sees the beginnings of modern European civilized development.

There had been civilizations before, such as that of Egypt (c 1450 B.C.), but the Greek civilization is of particular interest to the numismatist in that it produced

61

the first coins of the Western world. There had been coins in China at or before the same period as that during which coins first appeared in Greece, *c* 700 B.C., but because of lack of communication, the two developers of coins were not to meet for many centuries.

In these days of mass travel by air the collector can probably visit the modern bustling, dusty city of Athens. If he can get away from the tourists, he can contemplate the Acropolis and think back to the history that brought it into being.

The collector of Roman coins has a wider field of interest. He can trace the building of the Roman Republic and the Roman Empire through his collection. He sees an expanding world as the Romans pushed their conquests into Africa and Gaul, and as far as Britain itself. Unlike the Greeks, the Romans produced a more consolidated civilization over a long period of time. Eventually Roman rule and Roman law dominated the territories which were conquered, making them a Roman world.

If he is fortunate enough, the collector can visit Rome. In the midst of the busy, modern city he can see how the Roman architects made use of the arch, as opposed to the Greek beam, and how they used the arch to build such structures as the Colosseum, which itself is shown on contemporary coinage. This is but one single example of the advances in technology which the Romans made over the Greeks. If he cannot visit Rome or Italy, the collector will find that in almost any country of Europe he can trace the advance of Roman civilization. In Britain he can visit such places as *Verilamium* (St Albans), *Camulodenum* (Colchester), Hadrian's Wall (Northumberland), *Eboracum* (York) or the remains of the Roman Wall in London. Roman coins are dug up every year in Britain, sometimes in considerable quantities. As the modern tools of the developer go into action in Britain, more parts of the Roman Empire come to light.

The collector of the coins of any one country in Europe can see through his collection the development of that country. He can see how history repeats itself—how Europe, like Ancient Greece, consisted of a number of countries and states—and how they were combined or divided by war, finally settling into the Europe we know, itself still open to alteration and change. While any one generation may think it exists in a static geographical order of countries, this is not so. The order will change as the centuries pass. Changes in coinage will follow.

In Britain the numismatist can trace through coins the whole development of the country from pre-Roman times to the uniting of the various parts into the United Kingdom, to the building of the British Empire and to the conversion of that Empire into the British Commonwealth of Nations. On a broad basis this development can be divided as follows.

1 Ancient British coinage, *c* 125 B.C.–A.D. 40, both dates being very approximate. This early coinage was brought over from the mainland of Europe, largely by waves of refugees from Belgic Gaul, as the Roman conquests pushed towards the English Channel. Refugees are no new problem. The very crude design of this coinage was based on that of Philip II of Macedon, whose coinage was struck about the middle of the fourth century B.C.

2 Romano-British coinage. After the conquest of Britain by the Romans, completed by Claudius in A.D. 43—Julius Caesar had only carried out a couple of raids, in part to prevent the Britons from sending support to the Gauls—Roman coins were in circulation. Some were struck in Britain until the time of Constantius II (*ob.* A.D. 361). It is a matter of opinion whether such Roman coins should be part of the British collecting theme or if they should be confined to the Roman coinage theme.

3 Anglo-Saxon, *c* A.D. 575–775, with Viking coinages until A.D. 915. This is a complicated series emerging from the Dark Ages, when little if any coinage was in use in Britain. If any, it was probably that left by the Romans. The period covers the rough early issues and those of the kings of Northumbria, Kent, Mercia, East Anglia and Wessex, together with the issues of the Archbishops of Canterbury and York. The early ecclesiastical buildings, now in ruins, are close to the present cathedral in Canterbury and can be visited. Somewhere here was the Archbishop's mint.

4 The coinage of the first kings of all England, which covers the period 924–1066. There is no clear-cut point of change from the various Anglo-Saxon kingdoms to a united whole. The amalgamation was gradual. The first king of all England is usually taken as Edgar, who was crowned at Bath in 973, 14 years after succeeding to the throne. It will be noted that the period ends with the Norman Invasion of 1066 and covers the first part of the penny period already outlined. It was during this span of time that provincial mints proliferated.

5 Coinages of the Normans and Plantagenets, 1066–1272 (William I–Henry III). These coinages cover the remainder of the penny period, with the provincial mints still large in number.

6 The beginning of the expansion of English coinage, with the tentative introduction of the Groat and the establishment of a regular gold coinage. This period is between the reigns of Edward I (1272–1307)

and Charles II (1660–85). This immense period of some four centuries is of interest both historically and numismatically. A sophisticated England was emerging and with it a great growth in coinage. Attempts to produce a mill coinage occur at intervals, leading to the final extinction of hammered coinage in 1662. As has already been indicated, there are endless themes of collecting, the coinage of Charles I being but one example.

7 The introduction of mill coinage and its continuance until the present day. Another large period of some three centuries, during which English coinage became British coinage after the Act of Union with Scotland. Here, again, there are endless themes of collecting in all denominations and in metals from copper and bronze to silver and gold. Every theme is rewarding, however small or large it may be.

8 Before the Act of Union between England and Scotland in 1707 (Queen Anne, 1702–14), Scotland had a hammered and mill coinage of its own. This is a collecting theme on which many Scots, and Scots as far away from home as North America, specialize—a theme full of interest and colour, with cross-references to coinage in England.

9 Ireland also had its own coinage from early times. Between 995 and 1691 local mints were in operation. Later, Irish coinage was struck in Britain and exported. In 1826 the coinage of the United Kingdom was put into circulation. After the Anglo-Irish Treaty of 1921 Northern Ireland became joined with Great Britain in the United Kingdom. Modern Irish coinage was introduced in 1928 and still continues. Its design, featuring local fauna, was highly acclaimed. It is still in use and led the way to similar designs in the coinage of countries within the British Commonwealth of Nations.

10   During the latter part of this long period of time the British Empire, now the British Commonwealth of Nations, came slowly into being. Numismatically, many collectors take the Piece of Eight Testerns, issued as a trading piece in 1600 (Elizabeth I), with its subdivisions, as the starting-point of our 'colonial' coinage. This coinage was a failure. It was not accepted in trade in the Far East, where the Eight Reales of Spain had long been accepted as a trading piece. The story of the Spanish 'Piece of Eight' is a history in itself. For many centuries it was almost universally accepted in trade throughout the world.

The British Empire and Commonwealth was built up over some 300 years by discovery, by treaty or agreement, or by force of arms. Territorially, it reached its greatest extent during the nineteenth century. The Statute of Westminster of 1931 started the conversion of the Empire into the British Commonwealth of Nations, which developed gradually from this point. At the present time the Commonwealth covers some 14 million square miles of the earth's surface, embracing some 755 millions of people. The details of this great organization can be studied in *Whitaker's Almanack* and in the *Yearbook of the British Commonwealth*. With some 160 countries involved, there are naturally many collecting themes within the coinages of the British Commonwealth.

The divisions of coinage given above are simply suggestions. They attempt to bring a large subject into manageable proportions. Within each series almost unlimited themes of collecting exist. Works of reference will be found in the bibliography.

Since in this chapter the subject of coin collecting has dealt mainly with the coinages of the United Kingdom and the British Commonwealth of Nations, it might be of help to give some geographical details. Not a few collectors, especially in North America, find some difficulty in definition.

England: All the country south of a line from the Solway Firth to Berwick-upon-Tweed. Coinage struck within this area—which includes the Principality of Wales—can be called English coinage.

Scotland: All the country north of that line. Until the Act of Union of 1707 coinage struck north of the line is Scottish.

Ireland: The large island to the west of England/Scotland separated by the Irish Channel.

These three together form Great Britain, so called to distinguish it from Brittany in France. The area is also known as the *United Kingdom*. The Irish Free State, as Eire was originally called, seceded from this union in 1921, leaving only *Northern Ireland* within the United Kingdom. The UK also includes the *Channel Islands*, which became part of England at the time of the Norman Conquest, and the Isle of Man. Guernsey, Jersey and the Isle of Man have their own separate coinages and governments. British coinage is also accepted, as is Irish coinage in the Isle of Man. The Isle of Wight, Anglesey and the many islands around Scotland—such as the Inner and Outer Hebrides, Orkney, Shetland—the Principality of Wales and the Isles of Scilly have never had their own coinage.

Many of the 160 countries of the British Commonwealth of Nations have their own coinage. In the past, a number of them have accepted British money or any other coinage brought to them by international traders. It was the usual policy of the British government not to give an adequate supply of coinage in any form to 'the Colonies' until they were desperate for money. Nor was the local striking of money allowed. The trading nations brought all kinds of money with them, which came to be accepted. The complications of trying to equate these different forms of money can well be imagined.

Eventually, pressure of events in the localities forced the government to allow local coinage, sometimes struck at the Royal Mint, to come into being. Australia, Canada, South Africa and New Zealand, areas which were East and West Africa, Sarawak, Borneo, the Malay States, Fiji and many more eventually had their own coinage. Allowing for the changes in the coinage of certain territories and for separate coinages circulating in various states in one country (such as India) there are some 200 different series of coins within the area of the British Empire and Commonwealth available for study by the collector. Most of the more modern series are still reasonably inexpensive to collect. In every case a story of interest lies behind each issue, as well as behind the coinages which were accepted before local coins were introduced.

Quite apart from the interest and knowledge which a collector will acquire, any properly built collection of coins will, on past precedent, appreciate in value over a reasonably long term. The operative words are 'properly built collection'; what theme the collector adopts is only secondary in this connection. A brief glance can now be given to the investor collector, who only has appreciation in value, often in the short term, as his object.

The investor collector will buy any limited issue of modern coinage, irrespective of country, so long as he is assured of the limits of that issue. Such coins, gold and silver being the most popular, appreciate in value simply because they are limited in the actual number of specimens struck. They are controlled in order that there shall not be enough to meet the anticipated demand of the investor.

The investor will also buy 'coins' which may have little standing in actual fact, in that they were never intended for circulation. Such coins are frequently struck in gold, which he may not be able to buy or hold as a metal unless such metal is designated a 'coin'. Such issues as the present 'Krugerrand' are typical. So also are restrikes of gold coins long since demonetized.

President Kruger, in his time in South Africa, issued gold pound pieces, pounds, frequently and incorrectly called 'Kruger Sovereigns'. The present coinage of South Africa is based on a gold coin called the Rand. A combination of the two names produced the Krugerrand. It is a currency piece in South Africa but, like the present generation of British Sovereign, has a far higher value as bullion than it has in (nominal) circulation. Its value rises or falls daily, like company shares. With this type of gold coin the investor expects and frequently obtains a quick rise in the value of his investment. Unlike the company share the Krugerrand is an actual piece of gold and thus has a bullion value not accorded to a piece of paper. If all else fails the investor still has his gold, and cannot be blamed for that. The whole scene has been brought into being by the present economic climate of inflation and mistrust in investment as a whole. At the moment of writing, June 1976, there exists a buyer's market for the Sovereign and the Krugerrand. Both are purchased in many cases by 'loose' money. Better to hold gold than banknotes slipped under the mattress. When a seller's market develops, it is open to question what the investor will receive for his gold. On a seller's market the price will drop. Costs of essentials, food, clothing and shelter, will have risen while the investor held his gold. In these circumstances it will not buy him in essentials as much as his gold cost him. We are getting out of context: this is a matter for economists, not numismatists.

There is another type of coin which also appeals to the investor. He is offered specially struck proof pieces, limited in number but of a type also struck for normal circulation. When a coinage is first issued, or when any change is made in its design, even as small as the change in the date, it is at some mints the custom to strike a small number of such coins as proof pieces. They are highly polished, struck with great care and in perfect condition. Their original intention was to show the mint and the treasury authorities what the new coinage would look like, or that the change had been carried out correctly. From this came first the issue of proof sets of a new coinage for sale to collectors and later the issue of proof pieces, both in limited numbers. Later came issues of both in larger numbers simply for the investor to buy.

Several permutations can be and often are carried out. Suppose the State of Bogliwalla, which may be of long standing or only recently created, decides it will issue a coin of 50 pence face value for general circulation, struck in cupro-nickel. Seeing money to be made, the State announces that a limited number of proof pieces of the 50 pence will be struck in gold, a further number in silver and a large number in cupro-nickel. These proofs are offered at a premium price to investors and usually rise quickly in value. They are based on a coin which is in circulation and therefore legitimate. The profit from them may be pocketed by the State or may be devoted to a worthy cause. No one is deceived and the investor gets an appreciation on his capital outlay.

A recent example of this type of issue is the Conservation Coin Collection announced in 1974. The basic coins in this collection are money that will go into circulation. The proof pieces are for the investor. The profits will be devoted to the conservation of animals and birds which are in danger of extinction.

This is not really coin collecting as the numismatist knows it. But coin dealers with their living to earn cannot turn their backs on the investor and his money. Two unfortunate results have occurred. Tinkering with gold coinage for the investor is producing a growing crop of forged pieces, some of current coinage. Secondly, the backwash of investor collecting has played its part in forcing up coin prices in general. The same can probably be said of pictures and other art forms.

Some investor collectors become student collectors, but investor collecting should be viewed as an entirely separate form of coin 'collecting'. There is no reason why it should not continue, but it is not numismatics.

6

SELECTING AND CARING FOR COINS

Proof coins have been mentioned as perfect, specially struck examples of the coiner's art. Stemming from this, some advice on the selection and care of coins is now offered.

The student collector can collect coins in a variety of conditions. Unlike stamps—which when damaged are of no value—a coin can be in a number of conditions of preservation and still be accepted by the collector. A few simple, technical definitions may assist in the understanding of this statement.

Pattern coins   Such a coin is struck, usually one at a time, from polished dies on polished flans, from a design which is not accepted as suitable for a coin that will eventually be struck for general circulation.

When a new coin is under consideration many artists will submit suggestions for a design. Those which appear worthy of further consideration are sometimes translated from the drawing into an actual coin. At this point it may be considered that the design is unsuitable for a currency piece for one of many reasons. Alternatively, it may already be considered at the drawing-board stage that the design is unsuitable, but dies may be cut and a few specimens struck for the record, for sale to collectors or at the expense of the artist or minting authority. They may be struck some years after the submission of the design or after the date which appears on the coin. Such pattern pieces, struck long after their date, are known as 'later strikings' and are often difficult to detect.

Patterns are usually rare. As few as ten or less may be struck. Apart from those kept by the minting authority for the purposes of record, specimens will only appear on the open market at long intervals. They will usually pass from collection to collection. Apart from special circumstances which may vary the rule, they should be in absolutely perfect condition.

Proof coins   Much the same conditions apply as for patterns, save that a proof is struck to a design which is accepted for coins to go into general circulation. The origins of such pieces have already been given. Proofs are relatively more common than patterns, but can still be very rare.

Coins which go into circulation fall into various condition categories. Given that any one coin in a collection should be in the best possible condition obtainable, the following scale has been formulated.

FDC = *fleur de coin*, usually understood to signify a coin in mint state, plus a little more. Such a description can also apply to hammered coins which, because of their age, may be in mint or uncirculated state but have also attained with age a subtle patina or desirable atmosphere or apperarance. The distinction is hard to define: like certain old wines, such coins attain a bouquet.

Uncirculated   As soon as coins begin to be struck in quantity by mechanical means, some slight damage may be apparent from the moment they leave the machine. As the speed of striking has risen, this damage becomes more apparent. This is not because the machine produces a damaged coin but because, as the coins pour from the machine, they jostle and damage each other as they go. They are bagged into hundreds and sent out for circulation. They knock together and scratch each other, as the bags are tossed about. A mint is producing coins for use, not for collectors. So a coin may already have received major or minor damage even if it comes straight from the mint to the collector via a bank. It is still classified quite correctly as uncirculated. This word is often abbreviated to unc. in dealers' catalogues. If the coin is reasonably common the shrewd collector will examine as many specimens as possible before he finally selects the coin that he will add to his collection. More than this he cannot do. A small point is worthy of mention here. While the speed of the machines at the new Royal Mint at Llantrisant is of the highest order, the coins they are striking are in cupro-nickel, a very hard metal. The writer has before him a 5 pence, 1971, a 50 pence 1973 and a 10 pence 1974. All three are unc., are quite brilliant in finish and have sustained little or no damage at or since minting. The same could probably not have been said had they been struck in silver and on older machines.

EF. This is the next stage down the scale of condition in dealers' catalogues. A coin in *Extremely Fine* condition will have had an absolute minimum of circulation but will show some minor signs of wear. Unless it is a very common coin, such as a modern 50 Pence, it can be accepted by the collector as the best conditioned example he can obtain. Under the glass (the collector never buys without his magnifier in hand), it will show slight wear on the high points of the design, a little smoothing out of the monarch's hair or slight rubbing on the coat of arms or other device on the reverse. It is a highly acceptable piece to the collector.

VF, *Very Fine*, is next down the scale. Such a coin

24. Until the Act of Union, 1707, Scotland had its separate coinage. A gold ryal of Mary, Queen of Scots (1542–67), struck in 1555. It was equal to £3. (**11**.)

25. Ireland also has its separate coinage. A silver shilling of James I (1603–25) (**12**.)

26. James VI of Scotland (1567–1625) (James I of England). Gold hat-piece of 1591 so called for obvious reasons. It was equal to £4 (**12**.)

27. Silver halfcrown of Charles I (1625–49). The initial mark (P) shows it was struck during the Civil War by the Parliamentary side, who did not dare to introduce a new coinage till after the king's execution. Struck at the Tower mint, London. (**9**.)

28. Gold triple unite (=£3: III on rev.) of Charles I struck at his royalist mint at Oxford. The largest gold coin ever struck in the English series. The reverse contains the king's Declaration made at Wellington in 1642. (**9**.)

29. Silver halfcrown of Charles I. The plumes show it to be of Welsh silver and the BR below the horse to have been struck at a temporary mint at Bristol during the Civil War. (**9**.)

30. During the Civil War various towns and castles were besieged. They made their own money, mostly from domestic plate. A ninepence struck at Newark. OBS means *'obsidional'*; pertaining to a siege. (**9**.)

31. A similar piece from Pontefract Castle, a gold unite (£1). The obverse legend translates 'While I live I hope'. The blob on the left of the gateway is a defiant cannon. (**9**.)

32. A copper 17th-century token issued by the burgesses of Nottingham. (**13**.)

33. Copper halfpenny of Charles II (1660–85). After a long absence Britannia appears again (*see 7, ante*) here said to have been modelled by the Duchess of Richmond. (**14**.)

34. Hammered coins have now gone. A gold five guinea piece of Charles II, an early issue of milled coinage. The elephant and castle indicate that the metal was supplied by the Africa Company. (**15**.)

35. James II (1685–88) having a pecuniary interest in Cornish tin mines, then at a low state, caused tin halfpennies to be coined. As protection against counterfeiting a copper plug was inserted. (**14**.)

36. James VII of Scotland (II of England), silver forty shillings. (**11**.)

37. When James II fled to Ireland in 1688 his compatriots were soon short of money. Coins known as 'gun money' were struck from obsolete cannon and the like. This halfcrown (XXX=30 pence) was struck in September 1689.

38. A coin album, a modern method of keeping coins. A point to look for is strength at the page roots—coins are heavy.

will show definite signs of wear. To accept a coin in such condition presupposes it to be unobtainable in EF condition or to be more costly in that condition than the collector is willing to accept. Under these circumstances it is still an acceptable piece, but the standard of the collection as a whole may be lowered if too many VF coins are included.

F means *Fine* and is the next category below VF A coin in this condition will be quite badly worn by collectors' standards. It is only acceptable either as an inexpensive piece, or to fill the gap in a collection if no better piece can be obtained.

Below F, **M** for *Mediocre* and **P** for *Poor* were once used, while *Fair*, **VG** (*Very Good*) and **G** (*Good*) are also used for these lower grades. With the greater sophistication of coin collecting these descriptions have almost dropped out of use.

Combinations of the above, such as EF/VF, obverse extremely fine, reverse very fine, or EF–VF, general condition between the two, are sometimes used in the quest for accurate description. The collector will also come across 'almost EF', 'about EF' and similar designations such as GVF and GF, indicating Good, Very Fine and Good Fine, *i.e.* slightly better than VF or F.

These rules may seem hard, bearing in mind that a coin is an object of utility. They must be observed if the collector is to obtain the maximum satisfaction from his collection and if the collection is to maintain its value. They need not be too closely observed by the young collector who may have little money to spend. He has many years of collecting before him: he can improve his collection as time passes. He should not spend too much of his limited capital on worn coins, but certainly accept them if they are given to him to help his interest along.

Having put all this thought into the condition of coins the collector naturally asks if he should clean them. Really dirty coins are unsatisfactory, but cleaning should be undertaken with care. Basically, no method should be used which can damage the coin by friction or chemical deposit.

Copper and bronze coins are difficult to clean. If they are really dirty through, for example, long years under the soil, they will need special treatment and expert advice. Inexpert cleaning can cause verdigris to form. This is a sign that the metal itself is slowly disintegrating, a process which can rarely be arrested. Roman coins dug from the ground are frequently in this condition and are really only of academic interest, the find-spot and type of coin being then more important than the coin itself.

A bronze or copper coin which is just dull can be breathed on and then brushed with a soft brush. There are special soft brushes available, originally intended for the cleaning of domestic silver which also must not be scratched. Never use a nylon or man-made fibre brush: it will scratch. Note the type of discoloration. A bronze or copper coin may build up a patina with age which may be slightly enhanced by gentle brushing. Many Roman coins have such a patina and are greatly enhanced by it.

Silver and cupro-nickel coins *can* be cleaned with a little household ammonia and light brushing as indicated for copper, but are better left alone, and certainly must *never* be polished. Gold coins can be cleaned with a little mild acid, such as lemon juice, brushing as above. An alternative to the brush is a pad of cotton wool.

Coins in tin, brass, lead, mixed metals apart from cupro-nickel, and aluminium will be encountered. Unless any of these show signs of disintegration, in which case the collector should avoid them, a little brushing and breathing will do no harm. It is not necessary that an old coin should be brought back to the sparkling brilliance which it had on the day when it was struck. Respect, within reason, can be given to age.

More sophisticated methods of cleaning coins may be encountered. In expert hands they may be quite satisfactory. The collector should avoid them without expect advice. Examples have occurred of collectors brushing copper coins with light oil. However well this may appear to have been removed it still spreads around the collection. The coins always feel greasy and undesirable. Others have covered them with lacquer. This forms a thin skin on the metal and usually gives the coin an unpleasing colour. On balance the simple methods are best, with the overall consideration that the coins will normally be under frequent inspection.

Obviously there are many collectors in the world who have to keep their coins in bad atmospheric conditions. The damp of the tropics or industrial fumes will affect coins. These are special cases and advice should be obtained according to the local conditions. There are collectors of copper coins who would never think of smoking tobacco while the collection is being studied. This is indicative of the care with which a collection must be handled.

7

LOOKING AFTER YOUR COLLECTION

Coin albums fitted with transparent plastic pages each with a number of square pockets are now a popular way of housing a coin collection. Such an album must be strongly constructed; coins are heavy. The album can be placed on a bookshelf with normal books. This places the main weight of each page on the spring split rings which hold it. Look carefully at the method of construction of each page and the way it is held in the binder. The pages must not tear out at the roots.

Before coin collecting became a popular and general study collectors kept their coins in cabinets specially made for the purpose. Rising costs, shortage of good air-dried mahogany and lack of skilled craftsmen have made the coin cabinet an expensive object. Few are made except to special order. Those on the secondhand market are expensive.

Even so it is worth looking around for a cabinet. They are so specialized that you may well find one in a second-hand furniture shop or auctioneer's rooms. They may not even know what it is. Whatever its condition, buy it, provided it is not made of cedar or oak. You may well be able to repair or repolish it yourself, or get a tray or two made. Such repairs will be far less expensive than buying a new cabinet or having one made.

What in fact are you looking for? Coin cabinets come in any size from about one foot cube to that of a cupboard. Inside the main frame, say of about 20 in. wide by 10 in. deep by 12 in. high, are a number of thin trays, resting on runners. A few cabinets have, or have been adapted to have, trays resting on each other in a series of drawers. The bottom side of such trays should be padded, as they may rest on the coins below. Any cabinet with thin trays or small drawers should be inspected. It might be a coin cabinet.

The coin trays are pierced with a number of holes of various diameters to take coins. Square piercings are also sometimes met with. In both cases the piercings should be lined with felt or velvet to protect the coin from the wood. The trays should run easily. If they do not the coins will be shaken out and damaged.

Any cabinet made for, or adapted for, holding a coin collection should ideally be of mahogany or rosewood. Other woods contain too much water in various forms or, in the case of cedar and similar woods, too much oil. Either element will blacken silver and ruin copper. On the other hand a cabinet picked up in the saleroom may be of considerable age and be thoroughly dried out. You will have to decide this for yourself.

A few cabinets are now offered which are built of man-made plastic. Provided they are small they are quite satisfactory. Those seen contain about six or eight trays with padded square piercings, running in a light plastic framework. Such material is brittle and bends. Too large a coin cabinet in plastic will break or distort.

Many amateur cabinet makers have tried to make their own coin cabinets and have failed at one point. Having obtained the drills of various diameters to cut the piercings they have found that the wood with which they are working and in which they are cutting twenty or more holes breaks up as the drilling proceeds. If you try to make your own coin cabinet it is better to have square piercings built up from thin strip pinned or glued to an unweakened base. The use of such strip will need a lot of careful joining at the angles. Do not spoil your coin collection with a badly made cabinet.

You may think of other ways of keeping your coins which are quite satisfactory to you. Bear in mind the basic principles of care. Coins must not knock together, must not be piled one on another. They must be kept dry. Do not wrap them in newspaper in layers. If you keep each in an envelope, obtain special coin envelopes from a coin dealer. They are made of dried paper for this particular purpose. Plastic envelopes are usually all right to use, though in certain circumstances condensation can occur within the envelope since the material is quite unabsorbent.

8

COINS WHICH ARE LESS COSTLY

Early in this book it was shown how the coinage of this country could be broken down into a number of basic series, by age and in part by type. Most of those main series are very large. To collect on this scale is very expensive. Coins, as everything else today, have risen in price. Many potential collectors now feel that coin collecting is beyond their means. This is not necessarily so. This chapter will try to indicate a number of themes of collecting coins which are still within the means of the younger collector and of those who would limit the cost of their collection. A great deal has been said about collecting coins in precious metals, gold and silver. As world economics continue to run down, baser metals play an increasing part in the production of coins. Such metals must come within the collector's consideration. A coin is still a coin in whatever metal it may be struck and so has an interest to the collector. Let us look at some of the baser metals.

Aluminium at once suggests itself and presupposes an interest in modern coinage. In such coins many collectors had their first interest. Aluminium is not a metal dug from the ground it is pure state, like gold and silver; it is manufactured. It was named by Sir Humphry Davy in about 1812, was isolated by Wöhler in 1828 and then made slow progress towards mass production. Its manufacture is now carried out on a large scale with the help of reasonably cheap electricity, making it both common and relatively inexpensive. It does not rust if left unpainted and while light in weight it is strong. As an example of both these properties: in building the liner *Queen Elizabeth II*, launched in 1967, some 20 000 tons weight was saved by the use of aluminium in a ship almost the size of the *Queen Mary* (80 000 tons) built in 1935. Only the parts of the ship seen by the passengers had to be painted for decoration. The main structural parts would not rust and the metal was left in its natural state.

For coins of no intrinsic value, aluminium looked a likely metal in which to strike money. In Britain we have always had coins of a good substantial weight, after the hammered period. We still have such coins in cupro-nickel. We therefore tend to feel that any aluminium coins which we may come across in travel abroad are insubstantial. This does not deter the collector. Many countries have struck coins in aluminium: the British government was among the first to use this metal. In 1907–8 minor denominations were struck for East Africa and British West Africa. The alloy added to the metal caused it to deteriorate, if not rust, in the humid climate and the coins became unpleasant to use. In British West Africa the small coin valued at one-tenth of a Penny was cheaper to use as a builder's washer than the normal washer itself. Many of these coins thus disappeared into corrugated iron buildings. They may well be recovered many years from now; a new way of finding 'buried' coins.

But as soon as aluminium began to be produced in quantity at reasonably cheap cost, this with the rising cost of silver led to the production of a number of minor coinages. They increased after 1907, were given a boost by conditions after the First World War, and a further boost after the Second World War. Many of the countries of Europe, brought to the verge of economic ruin as a result of these two wars, cheapened their coinage and accepted aluminium, in some cases alloying it with bronze or other metals.

A theme of collecting exists here. So far few have recognized it, tending to despise such coins as mere tokens. In time to come, and coin collecting is always based on time, this may be regretted. Perhaps a parallel may be drawn with copper and bronze.

Pure copper as a coinage metal was in its turn despised by governments and collectors, as was aluminium. No sooner had Boulton received his contract for the copper coinage of 1797 than the price of the metal rose sharply. This brought to a halt further British coinage in this metal for some years. After an interval the metal came back into use—but the size, weight and cost of production dictated a change to bronze in 1860. This metal was later alloyed with nickel to produce, amongst many other pieces, the British 12-sided Threepence of 1937.

In Sweden in the eighteenth century attempts were made to produce copper coins of high exchange value. The result was Swedish 'plate money', large sheets of copper with value stamps at each corner and in the middle. Such pieces were too large for general use. If our 50 Pence contained that value of cupro-nickel the result would be the same. The story of Swedish plate money is a theme in itself.

When set against the values of coins in precious metals offered in dealers' catàlogues, copper and bronze pieces are still relatively inexpensive to collect. In all such statements of value exception must be made for the rarities in any metal. For various reasons, in any one decade, a year may be marked by very small production of any one coin. Coins are struck in anticipation of expected demand, bearing in mind the number in circulation. Thus a year may occur when, for example, few 50 Pence are needed. Only a small number may be struck. They are thus rare for this year and such rarities are always expensive.

Nickel as a coinage metal has a short history in so far as coins struck in the pure metal are concerned. Here Canada may be taken as an example.

When silver became too expensive for minor denominations, the Canadian 5 Cents was struck in nickel. This was in 1922, and a quite pleasing shiny, non-rusting coin resulted. The coin continued to be struck in nickel until 1936, the end of the reign of George V. Some minor varieties existed, but this series has long since been recalled and re-melted. The millions that were struck have almost disappeared.

Nickel 5 Cents continued, re-designed, from 1937 until 1941 (George VI), but by 1942 the metal was required for war purposes. Although some 6m+ coins dated 1942 were struck in nickel, 3m+ were also produced in Tombac, an amalgam of copper and zinc. By 1944 the 5 Cents were being struck in chromium-plated steel, giving a bright coin with a slightly blue tone. Nickel was again used from 1946 until 1951. In that year a commemorative 5 Cents was struck to mark the two-hundredth anniversary of the isolation of the metal. Paradoxically, in that year a shortage of nickel occurred and chromium-plated steel was again used. Nickel came back in 1955 and continues to be used to date (1976).

Meantime the 5 Cents, introduced as a silver coin in 1858, had passed through four reigns as a nickel piece, apart from those metals stated above. None was struck for the reign of Edward VIII, one of the four monarchs. There were a number of designs on the reverse, and two shapes—round and 12-sided. Though in total many millions of pure nickel 5 Cents are recorded as being struck, many have also been re-melted. A number of interesting varieties and rarities appear in the series. The 5 Cent piece of Canada has always been a pleasing little coin. It is still not too expensive to collect.

The ups and downs of pure nickel as a coinage metal can be similarly traced in other series of coins. Alloyed with copper it came into use in Britain in place of silver in 1947, giving us our present cupro-nickel coinage.

A collecting theme which has not so far been mentioned is token coinage. A token is not real money, but since most of the world's coinage at the moment has no intrinsic value it is all token money: a promise to pay.

In Britain in the seventeenth century there was a shortage of small change. Copper coinage could not or would not be struck by the Royal Mint. The country was unsettled with the Civil War and its aftermath, the Commonwealth and the rule of Cromwell. To meet the demand for small change, local traders, shopkeepers, inkeepers and the like had personal token coins struck for them. These were redeemed in various ways, usually at a slight loss to the person who cashed them. Since these tokens were personal issues showing the name and trade of the issuer as the legend, a great deal of local history can be traced through them. They became so numerous while the government did nothing to provide small change that they became almost legal. So much so that the seventeenth-century tokens are accepted by many collectors as a part of the coinage of the period. We have seen how the Penny in the Anglo-Saxon, Norman and later periods has an interest in that it names the town where it was struck and the moneyer who struck the coin. The seventeenth-century series of tokens has a similar interest. They named the issuer, the town in which he carried on his trade or business and what that trade was.

In the eighteenth century, before the government authorized Boulton to strike the copper Penny, a similar shortage of small change gave rise to another series of token issues. In form they resembled the regal Half-pennies to which reference has been made and which were being extensively forged. Boulton refers to the large number of such pieces which he obtained in change at such places as toll gates. He used this fact to bring to a head his campaign for a regal copper coinage.

Minting methods had advanced since the seventeenth century. The eighteenth-century tokens were well struck and frequently pictured local town buildings. There is a fine series of tokens depicting contemporary buildings in Coventry and a further series showing London buildings. But by this time the 'speculator' had begun to take a hand. Many tokens were struck specially to meet the interests of the collector and were not used as token money.

The eighteenth-century series thus needs care in its collection. It can be divided into the following categories—first set down by C. W. Peck in 1949.

Genuine trade tokens   Issued for the genuine purpose of providing small change: of good weight and with the name and address of the issuer.

Tokens for general circulation   Usually underweight, with no issuer's name. Sold by weight by the manufacturers at a good profit.

Advertising tokens   Of no stated value, but with the name, address and trade of the issuer. Frequently accepted by the public in change.

Tokens struck for sale to collectors   Not issued for 'money', but not without interest since they depict subjects of popular regard, such as contemporary buildings, zoological matters and the like.

Private tokens   These were often issued by token collectors themselves: they are few and rare pieces.

Forgeries   These are numerous and may constitute about 50 per cent of the varieties of the series.

The whole of this series has a collector interest, but the division given above must be known and understood.

In the early nineteenth century a shortage of money as a whole and of silver coins in particular gave rise to a further series of tokens. The Bank of England was forced by this shortage to issue Dollars and smaller denominations. These were overstruck on coins already in existence, such as the Spanish 8 Reales. This particular coin was also countermarked for general circulation with the head of George III in an oval or octagonal indent.

The same coin was also countermarked by many private industrial manufacturers and handed out to their employees as wages. Frequently they could only be cashed at shops owned or sponsored by the same manufacturer. Such places became known as 'Tommy shops' and the employee was frequently 'short changed'. A study of these tokens in great depth is being carried on at the present time, as there is still much to be learned about them. Such a study is indicative of the amount of research and interest the collector can carry out and find in any of the many themes of coin and token collecting.

While the seventeenth- and eighteenth-century tokens are still reasonably inexpensive to collect, some of the nineteenth-century series are expensive, since these countermarked pieces are now all rare. Being made from silver coins, large numbers of them have been melted down to recover the metal.

In this chapter we have been trying to indicate some

themes of collecting that are still reasonably inexpensive. One theme still remains for consideration.

In the nineteenth and early twentieth centuries large numbers of copper coins, many of them from France, were overstruck with legends intended mainly for purposes of advertisement. Such countermarks as PEARS SOAP, or LLOYD'S WEEKLY NEWSPAPER, are examples of some hundreds of such marks. Few people have collected or studied this series. They have a background history of no less interest than that of the seventeenth/eighteenth-century tokens. A guide book, dealing with this series in great depth, has just been published and will stimulate interest in a series so far neglected. It cannot be said of them that they are of any numismatic significance when set against true coins or tokens; but they are inexpensive to collect and at least give the collector guidance on how to study, research and follow up a theme of collecting.

39. A fine example of the Spanish silver 'piece of eight' which, for some 200 years was the accepted trading piece as world trade expanded (*see 23 ante*). (**16.**)

40. Irish halfpenny, struck during the reign of George I (1714–27). (**12**.)

41. When the Earls of Derby owned the Isle of Man, granted to the Stanley family in 1406, they struck a local coinage. Here a bronze halfpenny. A separate coinage for the island has recently been revived. (**17**.)

42. A copper halfpenny token issued in Manchester, 1793. (**13**.)

43. A Spanish silver eight reales countermarked for the Bank of England to circulate at 4/9d during a shortage of specie. It was undervalued. (**18**.)

44. Copper 'cartwheel' twopence of 1797, struck for the Royal Mint by Boulton's private mint at Soho, Birmingham. (**14**.)

45. Copper penny of 1806. (**14**.)

46. Bank of England 3/- token (*see* 43 *ante*).

47. The first of the modern generation of sovereigns. Designed by Pistrucci, the reverse shows the now accepted version of St. George slaying the dragon. (**15**.)

48. Set of silver Maundy money of George III (1760–1820). The same four coins are struck each year, still in silver, for the annual Maundy ceremony. (**19**.)

49 Gold pattern for a £5 piece, by William Wyon. Known as the 'Una and the lion' from the reverse device, it was considered too medallic for use as currency. (**20**.)

50. The so-called 'Gothic crown' of Victoria (1837–1901).
(**20**.)

51. Cupro-nickel coronation crown (5/-) of Elizabeth II (1952–) The queen is shown riding the horse 'Winston' at the annual ceremony of the Trooping of the Colour. Designed by Gilbert Ledward. (**10**.)

52. Set of Silver Maundy money as now struck. (**19**.)

53. The last type of the £ s d bronze penny. (**14**.)

54. The latest type of gold sovereign.

55. Cupro-nickel crown of 25p struck to mark the silver jubilee of the marriage of the Queen and Prince Philip, 1972.

9

HOW TO OBTAIN COINS

Collectors obtain their coins in various ways. Many a collection has been started by the finding or gift of a few coins which have sparked off an interest. Once started on collecting, some mention of sources of supply could be helpful.

The most obvious way to obtain coins is from a specialized dealer. There is one in almost every town of any size. How to judge the veracity of a coin dealer may need a little explanation. In Britain there are three leading coin dealers: Spink & Son, Ltd, founded 1666; A. H. Baldwin & Son Ltd, founded in the nineteenth century; and B. A. Seaby, Ltd, founded in the first quarter of the twentieth century. These three firms are all 'family' establishments, with descendants of the founder still in control. For many years they held the field almost exclusively. The beginner-collector should not be hesitant in dealing with them and in visiting their premises. They are established to help the collector of serious intent. He is always welcome and the collector should not feel 'put off' by their premises in the heart of the West End of London.

As coin collecting has increased, in particular since 1945, many other coin dealers have become established and the vast majority of them are equally reliable and interested in the collector and his needs. All of them have their reputation to protect and will not cheat the collector even though they realize that he is in the early stages of collecting. Many of them belong to an international organization founded to ensure honesty and fair dealing with the collector. Most of those in Britain also belong to a local trading association, which is also designed to ensure fair trading and to eliminate questionable business methods within the trade. The members of these organizations know all too well that sharp practice by unscrupulous operators can endanger the whole structure of the established coin dealer.

If you are considering collecting coins but have no idea how it should be done, the established dealer will gladly advise you, and will suggest possible themes of collecting which may be of interest. Take his counsel before you start collecting. Too much good money can be thrown away: too many potential collectors can become disillusioned by trying to collect without expert advice.

Once your theme of collecting has been established, the dealer will know which way you are going and will offer you coins on your theme. He will look out for them and advise you when he has coins in stock that are of your interest. He will probably put your 'wants' on an index. In the main, the coin dealer does not exist on passing trade—the person who drops in to buy a coin he has seen in the window. He is in touch with collectors on a world-wide basis, with collectors whom he may possibly never meet but whose interest he knows and provides for.

Most dealers will attend auction sales of coins and buy for the collector on commission, usually about 5 per cent of the price realized. Representatives of the leading dealers travel the world to attend sales and on buying and selling trips.

Auction sales are public functions. The collector may

go to look at the coins before the sale. Many auctioneers guarantee the authenticity of the coins being sold and may be prepared to cancel a lot sold if the coin is found to be false. This is a useful protection at this time, when forgeries and copies of interesting coins are on the increase.

If a collector wishes, he may attend the sale and buy his own lots. In this event he must know exactly what he wants and precisely how much he intends to pay. He will be buying against the dealers, who may carry large numbers of commissions for customers, and it is easy to get carried away by the competition among buyers. Most auctioneers sell on commission and will bid for a buyer without charge. The buyer must state his limit and most auctioneers will buy for him below that figure if possible. The complications of VAT should be studied by prospective buyers, and in some European countries there is a government tax on sales which must be taken into account.

The collector naturally likes to look around for coins from other sources, such as the general antique dealer. A possible 'find' may be made and this is a great attraction. The collector's theme should be well established before such buying is undertaken. A mass of miscellaneous coins may lay the foundation, but usually will not of themselves form a worthwhile collection.

Most general antique dealers have as a reference one or more of the catalogues issued by leading coin dealers giving the approximate value of coins in various series (*see* Bibliography). They are not now as ignorant on the subject of coins as they were forty years ago. The collector must therefore be well read on condition/price ratio and on rarity of the coins in his theme. He can then venture with some confidence into personal buying from various sources. There are still chances of bargains.

To obtain the fullest knowledge of a collecting theme, books are the obvious and most honest source. Highly academic works on the coinage of almost every country exist, from the coinages of Ancient Greece to those of modern times. While a number of publishers have produced catalogues of world coins from about 1750 to date, there is no world-wide catalogue containing everything issued from 700 B.C. to date. The subject is far too large ever to be contained in one volume. By numismatic standards stamps were only evolved yesterday and can thus be crammed into one large catalogue for use as a general reference, but coins cannot. The British Museum Catalogue of Ancient Greek Coins fills 29 volumes.

The output of books on coins is currently running at some two hundred a year, including reprints of earlier standard works. Nothing but a very selective bibliography can, therefore, be given in this book. Space will not allow detailed comment on them. It can be taken that the vast majority are fully illustrated or have representative plates.

BRITISH KINGS AND OTHERS, AND THE COINS ISSUED

THE PENNY PERIOD

Pennies alone were issued by the following and/or during the dates shown:

Kings of Kent
Heahberht (*c* 764)
Ecgberht (*c* 765–*c* 780 or later)
Eadberht Praen (796–8)
Cuthred (798–807)
Baldred (expelled in 825)

Archbishops of Canterbury
Jaenberht (766–92)
Æthelheard (793–805)
Wulfred (805–32)
Ceolnoth (833–70)
Æthered (870–89)
Plegmund (890–914)

Kings of Mercia
Offa (757–96)
Ceonwulf (796–821)

Ceolwulf (821–3)
Beornwulf (823–5)
Ludica (825–7)
Wiglaf (827–40)
Beorhtwulf (840–52)
Burgred (852–74)
Ceolwulf II (874–7?)

Kings of East Anglia
Beonna (*c* 758)
Æthelberht Lul (*obit.* 794)
Eadwald (*c* 796)
Æthelstan I (*c* 825)
Æthelweard (*c* 850)
Eadmund (855–70)

Viking Invaders, Anglia
Æthelstan II Guthrum (878–90/1)
Oswald (unknown)
'Halfdene' (*c* 900)

Northumbria (York)
'Sievert–Siefred–Cnut' (*c* 897)
Earl Sihtric (unknown)
'Raienalt' (*c* 910)

Hiberno-Norse Kings of York
Sihtric I (921–6/7)
Anlaf Guthfrithsson (939–41)
Anlaf Quaran Sihtricsson (926/7, 940–3, 949–52)
Sihtric II Sihtricsson (*c* 941–3)
Regnald II Guthfrithsson (941–3)
Eric (948, 952–4)

Kings of Wessex
Beorhtric (786–802)

Ecgberht (802–39)
Æthelwulf (839–58)
Æthelbald (855–60), no coins known
Æthelberht (858–65/6)
Æthelred I (865/6–71)
Ælfred the Great (871–99)
Edward the Elder (899–924/5)

Kings of All England (*Exact date and person still questionable, see* p. 64)
Æthelstan (924–39)
Edmund (939–46)
Eadred (946–55)
Eadwig (955–9)
Eadgar (959–75)
Edward the Martyr (975–8)
Æthelred II (978–1016)
Cnut (1016–36)
Harold I (joint King 1035–7, sole King 1037–40)
Harthacnut (joint King 1035–7, sole King 1040–42)
Edward the Confessor (1042–66)
Harold II (Jan.–Oct. 1066)

Norman Kings
William I (1066–87)
William II (1087–1100)
Henry I (1100–35)
Stephen (1135–54)

Plantagenet Kings (to 1272)
Henry II (1154–89)
Richard I (1189–99)
John (1199–1216)
Henry III (1216–72)

This ends the Penny period. It can be studied in great depth with the aid of North, *English Hammered Coinage*,

Volume I, *Early Anglo-Saxon c 650—Henry III, 1272,*
from which work the above lists are taken by kind
permission of the author.

We now come to the expansion of English
hammered coinage and it will be necessary to set it out
under the various denominations and metals issued
under each king.

Edward I (1272–1307)

Silver—Groat (tentative), Penny, Halfpenny, Farthing.

Edward II (1307–27)

Silver—Penny, Halfpenny and Farthing.

Edward III (1327–77)

*The coinage of this reign is divided into four sections, the
fourth of which is further sub-divided into three parts. (These
sections are known as coinage periods.)*

First coinage (1327–35)

Silver—Penny, Halfpenny and Farthing.

Second coinage (1335–43)

Silver—Halfpenny and Farthing.

Third coinage (1343–51)

Gold—Florin, Half-florin, Quarter-florin, Noble,
Half-noble and Quarter-noble.

Silver—Penny, Halfpenny and Farthing.

Fourth Coinage

First phase (1351–61), issued before the Treaty
of Brétigny (signed in Oct. 1360)

Gold—Noble, Half-noble and Quarter-noble.

Silver—Groat, Half-groat, Penny, Halfpenny and
Farthing.

Second phase (1361–69), issued during the Treaty
period

Gold—Noble, Half-noble and Quarter-noble.
Silver—Penny, Halfpenny and Farthing.
Third phase (1369–77), issued after the break-down of the Treaty
Gold—Noble and Half-noble.
Silver—Groat, Half-groat, Penny and Farthing.

The significance of the Treaty of Brétigny so far as the coinage is concerned is:

(a) Pre-Treaty—the King claimed the French throne by including REX FRANCIAE amongst his titles.

(b) Treaty period—the King replaced that title by that of Duke of Aquitaine.

(c) Post-Treaty—the title of King of France reappeared on the coinage. It continued to appear on English coins until George III (1760–1820), in spite of the fact that we had lost our last possessions in France some two hundred and fifty years before. To understand all this fully, some further reading on the history of the period is essential.

Richard II (1377–99)
Gold—Noble, Half-noble, Quarter-noble.
Silver—Groat, Half-groat, Penny, Halfpenny, Farthing.

Henry IV (1399–1413)
Gold—Noble, Half-noble, Quarter-noble.
Silver—Groat, Half-groat, Penny, Halfpenny, Farthing.
The coinage of this reign is divided into two: (1) Heavy coinage, issued 1399–1412, with the Noble weighing 120 grains and the Penny 18 grains. (2) Light coinage, the Noble weighing 108 grains and the Penny 15 grains. The Groat was not issued during the first period.

Henry V (1413–22)

Gold—Noble, Half-noble, Quarter-noble.
Silver—Groat, Half-groat, Penny, Halfpenny, Farthing.

Henry VI (1422–61)

Gold—Noble, Half-noble, Quarter-noble.
Silver—Groat, Half-groat, Penny, Halfpenny, Farthing.

Edward IV (first reign 1461–70)

Gold—Noble, Ryal, Half-ryal, Quarter-ryal, Angel.
Silver—Groat, Half-groat, Penny, Halfpenny, Farthing.

Henry VI (restored Oct. 1470–April 1471)

Gold—Angel, Half-angel.
Silver—Groat, Half-groat, Penny, Halfpenny.

Edward IV (second reign 1471–83)

Gold—Angel, Half-angel.
Silver—Groat, Half-groat, Penny, Halfpenny.

The story of how two of our kings managed to reign twice will be found in the history of the Wars of the Roses (1455–85), a story that would put most 'Westerns' into the background for arrogance, violence and bloodshed. Some of its memorials, such as that at Hadleigh Highstone (Barnet), still stand.

Edward V (1483)

Gold—Angel, Half-angel.
Silver—Groat, possibly also Half-groat and Penny.

The coinage of this reign is all doubtful. Edward was one of the 'Princes in the Tower'.

Richard III (1483–5)

Gold—Angel, Half-angel.

Silver—Groat, Half-groat, Penny, Halfpenny.

Henry VII (1485–1509)

Gold—Sovereign (name used for the first time), Ryal, Angel, Half-angel.

Silver—Groat, Half-groat, Penny, Halfpenny, Farthing. A Testoon, later to be called a Shilling, was introduced in this reign. It had, with the later issues of Groat and Half-groat, a fine profile portrait of the King. Profile portraits had rarely been attempted before this time.

Henry VIII (1509–47)

Gold—Sovereign, Half Sovereign, Angel, Half-angel, Quarter-angel, George Noble, Half George Noble, Crown of the Rose, Crown of the Double Rose, Crown, Halfcrown.

Silver—Testoon, Groat, Half-groat, Penny, Half-penny, Farthing.

The coinage is divided into three periods: First, 1509–26; Second, 1526–44; Third, 1544–7. Both gold and silver were heavily debased—that is, more alloy was added to the precious metal. Silver was so debased in the third period that the alloy showed through with a clear indication of the copper.

Edward VI (1547–53)

Gold—Sovereign of 30 shillings, Sovereign, Half Sovereign, Quarter-sovereign, Half-quarter-sovereign, Angel, Half-angel, Crown, Halfcrown.

Silver—Crown, Halfcrown, Shilling, Sixpence, Groat, Threepence, Half-groat, Penny, Halfpenny, Farthing.

The coinage is divided into four sections. The first coins still carried the name of Henry VIII. The coinage with the name of Edward VI is then divided: First period (2) April 1547–Jan. 1549; Second (3) Jan. 1549–April 1550; Third (4) 1550–3. A start was made with restoring the coinage to its proper metal content after the debasement by Henry VIII. This led to the first silver Crown (1551) and the silver (later cupro-nickel) range of coins as we knew them until decimalization, *i.e.* Halfcrown, Shilling, Sixpence, (Fourpence to come later), Threepence, (Twopence to come later), Penny, Halfpenny, Farthing (to disappear later in silver).

Mary (1553–4)
Gold—Sovereign, Ryal, Angel, Half-angel.
Silver—Groat, Half-groat, Penny.
It will be noted that only a few of the denominations of the previous reign were struck.

Philip and Mary (1554–8)
Gold—Angel, Half-angel.
Silver—Shilling, Sixpence, Groat, Half-groat, Penny.
As above, only a few of the possible denominations were struck.

Elizabeth I (1558–1603)
Gold—Sovereign of 30 shillings, Ryal, Angel, Half-angel, Quarter-angel, Pound, Half-pound, Crown, Halfcrown.
Silver—Crown, Halfcrown, Shilling, Sixpence, Groat, Threepence, Half-groat, Three-halfpence, Penny, Three-farthings, Halfpenny.
The hammered coinage is divided into three

119

periods: First, 1558–61; Second, 1561–82; Third, 1583–1603. Experiments with mill coinage produced: *gold*—Half-pound, Crown, Halfcrown; *silver*—Shilling, Sixpence, Groat, Threepence, Half-groat, Three-farthings.

James I (1603–25)

Gold—Sovereign, Half Sovereign, Rose-ryal, Spur-ryal, Angel, Half-angel, Laurel, Half-laurel, Quarter-laurel, Unite, Double-crown, Britain Crown, Thistle Crown, Crown, Halfcrown.
Silver—Crown, Halfcrown, Shilling, Sixpence, Half-groat, Penny, Halfpenny.
Copper—Farthing.

The coinage is divided into three periods: First, 1603–4; Second, 1604–19; Third, 1619–25. The silver and copper coins cover all three periods.

Though the two kingdoms were still separate, James I was the first monarch to rule both England and Scotland. The legends on the coinage reflect this, in that KING OF ENGLAND AND SCOTLAND, followed by KING OF GREAT BRITAIN, appear both in abbreviated Latin. The Unite took its name in part from the fact that it was a coin used in the two united kingdoms, though this unity was only in the person of the king, not in the administration.

As this is the last time that hammered coinages fell into more than one period, it should be pointed out that with the exception of the coinage of Edward III (where the issues are listed separately), the various denominations listed under the various periods were not all of them struck in each of such periods, nor were they struck in the order given. These apparent complications should not frighten the student.

We now enter upon the most complicated and interesting period of the hammered coinage, that of Charles

I. Due to the Civil War, mints were set up in provincial towns, as stated in the main text. Towns under siege also issued their own money.

At the beginning of the reign, the Royal Mint in the Tower struck money for the King. After the Civil War started it continued to issue regal-type coins, but for the Parliamentary side. The provincial mints then took over the work of providing money for the King. Of these mints, Aberystwyth struck coins before the War started (see p. 49). The various coins struck can be set down in a reasonably simple way as follows:

Charles I (1625–49)
From the Tower Mint
   Gold—Angel, Unite, Double-crown, Britain Crown.
   Silver—Crown, Halfcrown, Shilling, Sixpence, Half-groat, Penny, Halfpenny.
   Copper—Farthing tokens.

From York Mint, 1642–4
   Silver—Halfcrown, Shilling, Sixpence, Three-pence.

From Aberystwyth Mint, 1638–42
   Gold—Unite.
   Silver—Halfcrown, Shilling, Sixpence, Groat, Threepence, Half-groat, Penny, Halfpenny.

From Aberystwyth Mint, 1646 (or possibly from a mint at Coombe Martin, 1647–8)
   Silver—Halfcrown, Shilling, Sixpence, Groat, Threepence, Half-groat, Penny.

From Shrewsbury Mint, 1642
   Gold—Triple Unite (= £3, the largest English gold coin ever struck).

121

Silver—Pound, Half-pound, Crown, Halfcrown, Shilling.

From Oxford Mint, 1642–6
 Gold—Triple Unite, Unite, Half-unite.
 Silver—Pound, Half-pound, Crown, Halfcrown, Shilling, Sixpence, Groat, Threepence, Half-groat, Penny.

From Bristol Mint, 1643–5
 Gold—Unite, Half-unite.
 Silver—Halfcrown, Shilling, Sixpence, Groat, Threepence, Halfgroat, Penny.

From Truro Mint, 1642–3
 Gold—Unite.
 Silver—Half-pound, Crown, Halfcrown, Shilling.

From either Truro or Exeter Mint
 Silver—Halfcrown.

From Exeter Mint, 1643–6
 Silver—Crown, Halfcrown, Shilling, Sixpence, Groat, Threepence, Half-groat, Penny.

From Weymouth Mint, 1643–4
 Gold—Unite.
 Silver—Halfcrown.

From Sandsfoot Castle (near Weymouth), 1644
 Gold—Unite.
 Silver—Halfcrown.

From Weymouth or Sandsfoot Castle Mint
 Silver—Shilling, Sixpence, Groat, Threepence, Half-groat.

From Worcester Mint (probably located at Hartlebury Castle, near Kidderminster), 1646
 Silver—Halfcrown.

From Chester Mint, 1644
  Silver—Halfcrown, Threepence.

From an unknown mint
  Silver—Halfcrown

It is contended by some scholars that coins were struck on Lundy Island during the Civil War, but no documentary evidence has been found to confirm this. Silver Halfcrowns, Shillings, Sixpences, Groats, Three-pences and Half-groats sometimes attributed to Lundy—more probably came from Appledore, Barn-staple and/or Bideford. They have the mint marks A or B. Siege pieces were struck in the following towns:

Carlisle, besieged Oct. 1644–June 1645, coins struck May 1645
  Silver—Three Shillings (round), Shilling (round or octagonal).

Colchester, June–Aug. 1648
  Gold—Ten shillings (round).

Newark, besieged several times.
  Silver—Halfcrown, Shilling, Ninepence, Sixpence (all diamond-shaped).

Pontefract, besieged June 1648—March 1649
  Gold—Unite (octagonal).
  Silver—Two shillings (diamond), Shilling (diamond, round or octagonal).

Scarborough, besieged July 1644–July 1645
  Silver—Five Shillings and Eightpence, Five Shillings, Three Shillings and Fourpence, Three shillings, Two Shillings and Tenpence, Two Shillings and Sixpence, Two Shillings and Fourpence, Two Shillings and Twopence, Two Shillings, One Shilling and Ninepence, One Shilling and Sixpence, One Shilling and Fourpence, One Shilling and

Threepence, One Shilling and Twopence, One Shilling and One Penny, One Shilling, Elevenpence, Tenpence, Eightpence, Sevenpence, Sixpence, Fourpence.

Commonwealth (1649–60)

Gold—Unite, Double-crown, Crown.
Silver—Crown, Halfcrown, Shilling, Sixpence, Half-groat, Penny, Halfpenny.

Charles II (1660–85)

Hammered coinage (1660–2).
Gold—Unite, Double-crown, Crown.
Silver—Halfcrown, Shilling, Sixpence, Groat, Threepence, Half-groat, Penny.

All the above coinages can be studied in great depth in North, *English Hammered Coinage*, Volume 2, *Edward I, 1272–Charles II, 1662*, from which the details are taken with permission of the author.

This ends the complicated but most interesting hammered coinage of England. Many of its facets and problems are still the study of the collector and student.

Mill money, starting in 1662 as the national coinage, is far simpler to deal with. As will be seen from the following details, it falls into three main groups: Charles II–George III; George III—Elizabeth II; Elizabeth II decimal issues.

Charles II (1660–85)

Gold—Five Guineas, Two Guineas, Guinea, Half-guinea.
Silver—Crown, Halfcrown, Shilling, Sixpence, Fourpence, Threepence, Twopence, Penny—the last four now generally considered as Maundy Money.
Copper or tin—Halfpenny, Farthing.

124

56. Swedish 'plate money', 17th–18th century, copper. The idea was that these pieces should contain as much copper as their intrinsic value, in this case 8 daler. The result was a piece of metal of great size and weight. Smaller pieces were struck.

57. Silver cinquantina, Spain. The largest Spanish silver coin, value 50 reales. Another example of a coin so large as to be useless, measuring 4½ in. in diameter.

58. Not really a coin, this bar of gold, stamped for authentication by Spain was another method, like no. 57, of transporting great wealth of gold and silver from the New World. Of great rarity, this bar was recovered from a wrecked galleon in recent times.

59. Gold French 40 franc piece of Napoleon as emperor, 1812—the year of his retreat from Moscow. (**22**.)

60. Siam, gold 8 tical, or bat, 1864, early European-type coinage of king Mongkut (1851–68). (**23**.)

61. Aluminium 1/10th penny of British West Africa, 1907. The Royal Mint was the first in the world to strike coins in this, then not common, metal. (**24**.)

62. A bronze French 'penny' overstamped to advertise Pears
Soap, one of many coins so used. (**25**.)

63. The Canadian 5 cent piece, the first issue in nickel, 1922.

64. Gold so-called pattern 5 marks of 1927, showing President von Hindenberg, designed by Karl Goetz. (**26**.)

65. Republic of China, 1911–49, silver 'one dollar' 1928. A traditional obverse with a modern reverse. (**27**.)

66. China (Formosa), 2000 yuan piece, 1966, commemorating the eightieth birthday of Chiang Kai-Shek.

67. The last of the Egyptian kings, 500 piastres of King Farouk (1937–52).

James II (1685–8)
The same denominations.

William and Mary (1688–94)
The same denominations.

William III (1694–1702)
The same denominations, but no coins in tin.

During this reign the last of the hammered coinage was called in and melted. Temporary mints were set up in Chester, Exeter, Norwich, York and Bristol to strike silver coins in an attempt to meet the demand. There were no Crowns from these mints; the Half-crowns, Shillings and Sixpences carry the initial letter of the mint below the bust. There are almost endless varieties. They are dealt with in detail in a monograph, *Some Notes and Observations on the Silver Coinage of William III*, by E. R. Jackson Kent (Spink).

Anne (1702–14)
The same denominations, but only Farthings in copper.

Some of the gold and silver coins have the word VIGO below the bust, showing that they were struck from metal captured at the Battle of Vigo Bay. Of the Five Guineas so struck, only about 15 are thought to exist, making it the rarest of the English coins of this denomination. During the reign, the act of Union with Scotland ended the separate Scottish coinage. English coinage now became British coinage.

George I (1714–27)
The same denominations, with a Quarter Guinea in gold and Halfpenny and Farthing in copper.

George II (1727–60)

The same denominations, but no Quarter Guinea.

George III (1760–1820)

First period, 1760–1816, struck at the Town Mint.

Gold—Guinea, Half Guinea, Third Guinea, Quarter Guinea.

Silver—Shilling, Sixpence, Maundy Money, Bank Dollars and smaller denominations struck for the Bank of England to provide silver coinage in the shortage of regal issues.

Copper—Penny, Halfpenny, Farthing.

Second period, 1816–20, struck at Tower Hill Mint.

Gold—Sovereign, Half Sovereign.

Silver—Crown, Halfcrown, Shilling, Sixpence, Maundy Money.

(The Tower Mint, the Tower Hill Mint, and Llantresant Mint to come, are now usually referred to as The Royal Mint.)

George IV (1820–30)

Gold—Two pounds, Sovereign, Half Sovereign.

Silver—Crown, Halfcrown, Shilling, Sixpence, Maundy Money. (While the silver Threepence circulated from about this period, the three other pieces did not.)

Copper—Penny, Halfpenny, Farthing. There were also Half and Third Farthings, but these circulated in Ceylon and Malta respectively. Collectors will come across them.

William IV (1830–7)

Gold—Sovereign, Half Sovereign, the latter in two sizes.

Silver—Halfcrown, Shilling, Sixpence, Groat (with

Britannia on reverse, as distinct from figure 4 on Maundy Groat). Maundy Money.

Copper—Penny, Halfpenny, Farthing (also Half and Third as above).

Victoria (1837–1901)

Gold—Five Pounds, Two Pounds, Sovereign, Half Sovereign. (The two large pieces saw little circulation and were struck only in 1887 and 1893.)

Silver—Crown, Double Florin (=4/–), Halfcrown, Florin (=2/–), Shilling, Sixpence, Groat, Threepence, Maundy Money. The Britannia Groat ended in this reign. Large numbers of Threepence, similar to the piece used in Maundy Money, were struck for general circulation.

Copper (later bronze)—Penny, Halfpenny, Farthing, Third Farthing for Malta.

The coinage falls into three types, usually designated 'Young head', 'Jubilee head' and 'Old head'. There were also coins known as 'Gothic' Crowns and Florins, all current and with the date in Roman figures. They are sometimes designated a fourth type. There were no Jubilee head coppers. Copper became bronze in 1860.

Edward VII (1901–10)

Gold—Five Pounds, Two Pounds, Sovereign, Half Sovereign. (The two large gold pieces again saw little if any circulation. In revising the *Handbook of the Coins of Great Britain and Ireland in the British Museum* the author accidentally stated that the Five and Two Pounds only existed as proofs. This is not correct; there were ordinary pieces, for the last time.)

Silver—Crown, Halfcrown, Florin, Shilling, Sixpence, Threepence, Maundy Money.

Bronze—Penny, Halfpenny, Farthing, Third Farthing for Malta.

George V (1910–36)

Gold—Sovereign, Half Sovereign. (Five Pounds and Two Pounds only struck as proofs in 1911. The collector may come across a small gold coin struck in the Middle East and known as a Quarter Sovereign. No such official coin has ever existed in our milled coinage.)

Silver—Crown, Halfcrown, Florin, Shilling, Sixpence, Threepence, Maundy Money. When the silver coinage was re-designed in 1927, the non-Maundy Threepence was given its own design. Silver was debased for the first time for 400 years in 1920.

Bronze—Penny, Halfpenny, Farthing.

Edward VIII (1936, 20 Jan.–11 Dec.)

No coinage was issued for circulation in Britain. Experiments for a new Threepence in nickel-brass were being carried on. A few 'escaped' from the Royal Mint, but the collector is not likely to see one. See *The Proposed Coinage of Edward VIII* by G. P. Dyer. (HMSO). Some minor denominations without the King's portrait circulated in East Africa, British West Africa, New Guinea and Fiji.

George VI (1937–52)

Gold—none. The four gold pieces were struck as proofs in 1937. Sovereigns were struck from reserve gold in 1949, 1951 and 1952 but were from dies dated 1925. see *Sovereigns of the British Empire* by J. J. Cullimore Allen (Spink).

Silver—Crown, Halfcrown, Florin, Shilling, Sixpence, Threepence, Maundy Money.

Cupro-nickel—Crown, Halfcrown, Florin, Shilling, Sixpence.

Nickel-brass—Threepence (12-sided).

Bronze—Penny, Halfpenny, Farthing.

136

With the introduction of cupro-nickel the silver Maundy Money was restored to the original fineness of 925 parts in 1000. It so continues.

Elizabeth II (1952–)

Gold—none. Sovereigns were in fact struck in 1957 and in a number of other years until the present. Though they are still legel tender at £1, the price (1975) fluctuates around £30. They are used as 'bullion'; the inhabitants of some Middle East countries still hold Sovereigns as personal savings. The four gold pieces were struck as proofs: only about five sets may exist.

Silver—Maundy Money.

Cupro-nickel—First period, from Tower Hill Mint. Crown, Halfcrown, Florin, Shilling, Sixpence.

Nickel-brass –Threepence.

Bronze—Penny, Halfpenny, Farthing. The Farthing was last struck in 1956.

Cupro-nickel—Second period, from Llantrisant Mint. Fifty New Pence, Twenty-five New Pence, Ten New Pence, Five New Pence. (A Twenty-five New Pence of original Crown size was struck to commemorate the silver wedding of the Queen and Prince Philip in 1973. A similar piece was struck to commemorate the silver jubilee of the Queen's reign in 1977.)

Bronze—Two New Pence, One New Penny, Half New Penny.

BIBLIOGRAPHY

References to Figure Captions

The following works are referred to in the captions by means of the bold numerals. Some of these titles are now out of print (indicated by the letters o.p. in this list) but they can often be obtained second-hand or from reference libraries.

 1 *Pepys' Diary*, 1662
 2 Shepperd and Musham, *Money Scales and Weights* (Spink)
 3 Vermeule, C. C., *Some notes on Ancient Dies and Coining Methods* (Spink, o.p.)
 4 Mack, R. P., *The Coinage of Ancient Britain* (Spink)
 5 Mattingly, H., *Roman Coins* (Spink, reprinting)
 6 Seltman, C. T., *Masterpieces of Greek Coinage* o.p.
 7 Brooke, G. C., *English Coins* (Spink)
 8 North, J. J., *English Hammered Coinage* Volume 1 (Spink)
 9 North, J. J., *English Hammered Coinage* Volume 2 (Spink)
10 Linecar, H. W. A., *Crown Pieces of Great Britain and the British Commonwealth of Nations* (Spink)
11 Stewart, I. H., *The Scottish Coinage* (Spink)
12 Dowle, A. and Finn, P., *The Guide Book of the Coinage of Ireland* (Spink)
13 Dalton and Hamer, *The Provincial Token Coinage of the Eighteenth Century* (Seaby, o.p.)
14 Peck, C. W., *Copper, Tin & Bronze Coins in the British Museum, 1558–1968* (British Museum Publications)
15 Linecar, H. W. A. (editor) *The Milled Coinage of England* (Spink)
16 Yriarte, J. O., *Catalogo de los Reales de a Ocho Esanolas* o.p.
17 Pridmore, F., *The Coins of the British Commonwealth of Nations* Part I (Spink)

Berry, G. (1974). *Medieval English Jetons*, Spink & Son, Ltd.

Dalton, R. (1922). *The Silver Token-Coinage, 1811–1812*, B. A. Seaby, Ltd.

Davis, W. J. (1964). *The Nineteenth Century Token Coinage*, B. A. Seaby, Ltd.

Davis, W. J. and Waters, A. W. (1922). *Tickets and Passes*, Spink & Son, Ltd.

Scott, J. G. (1975). *British Countermarks on Copper and Bronze Coins*, Spink & Son, Ltd.

Williamson, G. C. (1967). *Trade Tokens issued in the Seventeenth Century*, 3 vols, B. A. Seaby, Ltd.

This bibliography only touches the surface of the great amount of numismatic literature available. An annual catalogue of books on every phase of coin collecting, entitled *About Those Coins*, is published by Spink & Son, Ltd, and is available free on request. All the books listed can be obtained from Spink; those out of print are searched for.

INDEX

NOTES